Talking About Lobsters

NEW WRITING SCOTLAND 34

Edited by
Gerry Cambridge
and
Diana Hendry

Gaelic adviser:
Rody Gorman

Association for Scottish Literary Studies

Association for Scottish Literary Studies
Scottish Literature, 7 University Gardens
University of Glasgow, Glasgow G12 8QH
www.asls.org.uk

ASLS is a registered charity no. SC006535

First published 2016

British Library Cataloguing in Publication Data

A CIP record for this book is available
from the British Library

ISBN 978-1-906841-26-3

The Association for Scottish Literary Studies
acknowledges the support of Creative Scotland
towards the publication of this book

ALBA | CHRUTHACHAIL

Printed by Bell & Bain Ltd, Glasgow

CONTENTS

INTRODUCTION

There's a passage in one of Isak Dinesen's novels in which she imagines that in the process of dying she might see the shape and meaning of her life mapped out in stars. Receiving the proofs of this, the thirty-fourth issue of *New Writing Scotland*, I find myself holding my breath to see if, now that all these stories and poems come together, the zeitgeist of Scotland will be revealed – or, at least, the themes most preoccupying its writers.

I can't claim to be any wiser as to the zeitgeist, but I'm relieved to find that the subject of borders, and the difficulty and fear of crossing them, has got into the psyche, most notably in Uilleam Blacker's story 'Crossing the Line' and Morelle Smith's travelogue 'Tibor on the Train'. Elsewhere, the dominant theme is that of fathers and sons – ageing fathers, missing fathers, abandoned sons, illegitimate sons, lost and troubled sons – and sheep. This is the year when, poetically, sheep get a makeover. There's Hugh McMillan's sheep, seen in the hills 'hanging in space on their stilt legs', and Graham Fulton's – 'Afraid of everything, / but not knowing what anything / is'. Bless 'em!

This being my second year as co-editor with Gerry Cambridge, I've found myself increasingly obsessed with the question, 'how to define a good short story?'

It seems much easier with a poem. At its simplest, a poem is either alive or it hasn't made it. There are lots of very good, very readable short stories, but few that reach that pitch of excellence to rank with Chekhov, Joyce, Carver, MacLaverty. Perhaps it has to do with memorability.

The wonderful Irish writer Claire Keegan's mantra is that 'a story is about something of consequence happening to somebody' and that there are three kinds of conflict: man versus the environment, versus man, versus himself.

And then, of course, there is the beginning and ending of a short story. A good first line is a winner for me. In this collection, the title story's opening – 'The lobsters walk at night, their ten stubby legs lumbering over gravel and sand' – has me immediately hooked. As for endings, I'm fond of R. K. Narayan's thought that an ending should produce either a revelation or a resolution. Chekhov's rarely do either, but then that's Chekhov.

The range of stories within *Talking About Lobsters* encompasses crime, fantasy, history, school, diary and dialogue forms (the latter including a long conversation with a rather intransigent satnav).

As for the poems – lyrical, witty, elegiac and narrative – we believe all to be alive and quickened by whatever you like to call it: inspiration, the muse, magic, language itself.

This is Gerry Cambridge's last year as co-editor of *New Writing Scotland*. It has been a great pleasure and an education working with him. His more than twenty years as editor of *The Dark Horse* has given him a fine editorial instinct and a commitment to what he regards as the very best writing. Perhaps too, he's grown a thicker skin, for it still pains me to reject both stories and poems which, given more space, might have made it. Most of the time, Gerry and I were in agreement. Only a little bartering was needed!

And finally, I'm amused to find that this year's collection opens with a poem on the sense perception perhaps least written about.

Diana Hendry

NEW WRITING SCOTLAND 35: SUBMISSION INSTRUCTIONS

The thirty-fifth volume of *New Writing Scotland* will be published in summer 2017. Submissions are invited from writers resident in Scotland or Scots by birth, upbringing or inclination. All forms of writing are welcome: autobiography and memoirs; creative responses to events and experiences; drama; graphic artwork (monochrome only); poetry; political and cultural commentary and satire; short fiction; travel writing or any other creative prose may be submitted, but not full-length plays or novels, though self-contained extracts are acceptable. The work must not be previously published, submitted, or accepted for publication elsewhere, and may be in any of the languages of Scotland.

Submissions should be typed on one side of the paper only and the sheets secured at the top left corner. Prose pieces should be double-spaced and carry an approximate word-count. **You should provide a covering letter, clearly marked with your name and address.** *Please also put your name on the individual works.* If you would like to receive an acknowledgement of receipt of your manuscript, please enclose a stamped addressed postcard. If you would like to be informed if your submission is unsuccessful, or would like your submissions returned, you should enclose a stamped addressed envelope with sufficient postage. Submissions should be sent by **30 September 2016**, in an A4 envelope, to the address below. We are sorry but we cannot accept submissions by fax or email.

Please be aware that we have limited space in each edition, and therefore shorter pieces are more suitable – although longer items of exceptional quality may still be included. **Please send no more than four poems, or one prose work.** Successful contributors will be paid at the rate of £20 per published page. Authors retain all rights to their work(s), and are free to submit and/or publish the same work(s) elsewhere after they appear in *New Writing Scotland*.

ASLS
Scottish Literature
7 University Gardens
University of Glasgow
Glasgow G12 8QH, Scotland

Tel +44 (0)141 330 5309
www.asls.org.uk

James Aitchison

SMELL

From our first house to my first full-time job
I sometimes walked to work along farm roads.
In June the fields of broad beans blossoming
smelt like the kind of perfume a man could wear.

A neighbour gave me a bucket of pig's blood:
'Fertiliser. For your vegetables.'
I left the bucket in the greenhouse.

Two days later when I opened the door
the smell of butchery and sacrifice
bypassed my frontal lobes
and fired the reptile neurons in my brain.

When I was a lizard my breath was poisonous.
I could sniff out
the farthest whiff of putrefying flesh.

Brown-tipped matchsticks like little Bengal lights
have cauterised both nostrils' nasal veins.
I cough and snotter small gobbets of congealed blood
and for a day or two I lose my sense of smell.

A perfumed man?
I suppress groin and armpit pheromones
with an invisible deodorant.

Ruth Aylett

NOTHING TO TELL

You all right? Did them big boys hurt you? I'll not have them bullying my little brother . . .

Okay, okay, I know six isn't that little. Okay, not little at all.

Don't worry about that, it's just a bit of mud on your trousers, it'll brush off. Look, you've been on the common playing before, what's the problem?

Yes, it will brush off. When it's dry. Doesn't hardly show.

It wasn't much of a puddle anyway. Come on, blow that nose, you're fine.

Just wait while I do my button up, always hurts my fingers. Why do they put these nasty metal buttons on jeans?

It's undone coz I was wrestling, wasn't I? With that boy. You heard him – he said girls couldn't wrestle. See who's stronger. But you know I can wrestle really well, must have come undone then.

Nah, wasn't screaming – bet you've never heard anyone really scream or you wouldn't think that.

Them? They was just his friends, thought it'd be a bit of a laugh to drag me into their den. Yeah, under that tree where the branches come down. Private den, that's why they wouldn't let you in.

I can't help it if my trainer hit you in the face – it must've fallen off and someone chucked it. Wasn't me, one of them.

Look, stop fussing, it's only mud. Let me see if I can brush it off now. I can do your face with my hankie, just let me get a bit of spit. Nah, your nose really isn't bleeding.

Well, if you hadn't tried to get into their den they wouldn't have shoved you like that, would they? And it wasn't much of a puddle.

What was they doing to me? Nothing.

Okay, they tickled me, see, that's what all the noise was. You know I don't like being tickled, so I was telling them to get off. That's what you heard. That's not screaming, that's just telling someone to get off. And they did, didn't they? And here I am.

Right, that's your face done. Now just let me get my button done up.

Yeah, my face is fine.

No, those aren't tears, just all that wrestling made my eyes water.

Can you see if I've got leaves on my back?

So brush them off then.

And why are you crying? I'm fine. I really am fine.

But don't tell Mum. Because there's nothing to tell.

Nothing.

Pamela Beasant

LERWICK, AND LISE

Walking in Lerwick
haunting your steps

you're here
in this place you knew

these stones, streets, windings;
it reproduces

the turn of your face
glimpsed ahead

teasing, smiling
disappearing,

a vivid gap,
as the steel blast

still winter-edged
numbs the brain

hits the eyes,
makes them run

run on this day
continuing

all the days of the world
unknown.

Simon Berry

SCOTCH PUMICE[1]

Magma, feggs!
Ah niver thocht ah'd thole it
Stickit in that mou' o' riftin wambles –
Then wi' a volcanic voamit
    Ah wis makt free.[2]

                Syne feelin glewy
          Frae sic a flamin het emission:
      Nou rinnin doon the brae all canty
          Next a' lag wi' deein passion
             Ah sensed a shift.[3]

No sae het the nou:
Jist like it is wi' a marriage
Frae a braw lava burn transformit
Tae a platter o' cauld parritch.
    Ah'm made a' wabbit.[4]

                Unco cauld stane
          A' droukit ah must dree it –
      Tae scrape my leddy's nou ma job.
         Yet aiblins ah can see in it
          Ain antisyzygy.[5]

NOTES

1 Orig. title 'Ma Leddy's Pumie[*sic*]-Stane's Lamentation' (prob. indecent).
2 That magma! / I never thought I'd withstand / being stuck in that mouth that's belching and roaring – / Then with a volcanic regurgitation / I was freed.
3 A while ago I was in a viscous state / due to the heat of the emission: / One moment flowing cheerfully downhill / the next I became sluggish as / I sensed a change and my feelings diminished.
4 Not so hot at this very moment: / just like in a marriage / when passion goes from a lively stream of burning lava / to a dish of cold porridge. / Just so I've become exhausted.
5 Turned to awfully cold stone / I must bear being drowned – / for I'm now occupied in exfoliating my mistress. / Even so I can detect here / a potential yoking together of opposing ideas.

Uilleam Blacker

CROSSING THE LINE

Whenever I get near a border I feel tense and my stomach churns. It's like I can smell it, the nauseating smell of the border. It's like feeling seasick. Because you know that they are waiting for you: the one without the piece of paper, because you were born on the wrong side of a line on a map. And here we are heading for another one, and I feel sick, and it has nothing to do with the car.

I've been watching the landscape change through the window as we go north, from flat land and endless town, to leaves and brick houses, then the more dilapidated, more grey places, long flat cities; a lot of motorway; then some hills and stone walls, long all across the hillsides, which it must have taken years to build – quite some effort just to keep in a few sheep, those little white clouds that look as if you could just blow them over the walls with a light puff of your breath; and now these hills with darkening clouds nearer the border. The other two seem fine. I don't know why, especially O., who is in no better a situation than I am, with no documents; she looks over her shoulder and smiles a big smile and offers me another crisp or biscuit or something that I can't face eating. And why shouldn't she smile? We're going on holiday after all – it'll be the first time I've crossed a border just to go on holiday. But all the same, I still feel sick.

Borders are like those stupid Russian dolls: those gaudy little wooden things they sell in Ukraine even though it's nothing to do with us. There's the border between Ukraine and Poland; which is also the border between the EU and the Rest of the World, and it's also the border of the Schengen zone, the sacred Schengen zone, whose visas carry you across the continent like a magic carpet. And then inside that there are more borders: Poland–Germany–France; or you can go Poland–Czech–Germany–France; or maybe Poland–Germany–Netherlands–Belgium–France. Of course, that's not really a problem any more, at least not like it would have been before. Because there's no control. If you pay attention you can see the old border posts, some are even empty and overgrown. So nice – the old bad history buried in the ground, feeding the plants, and no more iron curtains. That's how it is inside Schengen, that fairy-tale land, with its overgrown castles.

Our border crossings are still in business, of course. Business being the operative word. A licence to rake it in from all the trucks and lorries, the smugglers and the illegals. Just sit there, put your feet up, practise your sceptical face and hold out your hand. You can sit for hours on our border. They take their cut. They haul you out and ask you pointless questions and take turns to squint at your passport until you give in and slip them the cash. I know that, in the end, it's not the worst border to get across. You see those women in the queue taking alcohol and cigarettes over, and they've done it a million times, and they take it in their stride. But I get sick every time. Maybe it's the uniforms, the tired, cold faces, the dogs, I don't know. But I get it every time.

There are various ways to get over our border into Poland, of course. You can drive, but that means the worst queues, and they might take your car apart screw by screw just to check you've not hidden anything or anybody in there. Or you can go on foot, which I prefer. You take the minibus to the village near the border crossing and then just walk. Last time I went the bus was full of gypsies, singing all the way through their gold teeth, which didn't help me relax one bit, with their chickens in baskets on their laps. Seriously, this is the difference: not even Poles take chickens on a minibus any more, but we do, and not just the gypsies. And the Poles have a lot fewer gold teeth. That's the difference between Europe and Noteurope; outside the Schengen border it's all gold teeth and chickens.

And so you queue, and when the Ukrainians eventually let you through, you walk down this long corridor between two high fences with barbed wire, and combined with the dogs it makes you feel as if you're being released from some prison camp. And off to each side there's this big strip of empty land, this nothing, this no-man's land, like between two trenches. A dead place, bogs and nothing.

And then you have to deal with the Poles speaking loudly to you in Polish as if it was the lingua franca of the EU: and you're meant to understand, aren't you, learn from big brother . . . But they are just as bad: they know what we are up to, and we know they know, and you see this charade, this pantomime that happens every single day, those women standing there with their fags and spirits strapped to themselves in every nook of their bodies and the Polish border guards lording it, looking at them as if they were naughty children and wondering which one to make an example of in front of the class; except it's not like that, because they're taking backhanders from those women. And the women laugh at them when they're gone.

Or you can always take the train over the border. It takes several hours on our lumbering, cumbersome train to trundle to the border from L'viv along our wide, sleepy, slow rails, even though it's only eighty kilometres. Our trains are like us – not built for life in Europe. They can go over the border – but only just. Because the wheels aren't right for Europe's slim, polished rails. Only for our fat, iron ones, like peasants' fingers. Our trains would fall over like a drunk on the dainty European railway lines. So they let us in a bit, just enough to get to Przemyśl and sell whatever it is we've stuffed up our jumpers and then go back again.

The smugglers like the train: first they get out their lunch, all wrapped in greasy towels and newspaper, their tomatoes and boiled eggs and sausages and they laugh and plot. And then when they've got some fuel inside them it starts: those big checked plastic bags, blue and red ones, made in China – when they bury Ukraine they'll wrap it in one of those and throw it in the ground – the manic rustling of bags and plastic and paper, blocks of fags, unwrapping the foil, breaking them up. And Sellotape! Sellotape screeching and stretching and strapping it all to themselves, to their big sweaty, warm bodies; middle-aged women hike up their blouses and t-shirts and strap the fag packets in; and the vodka too – spirits into bags and into the bra. It's quite an operation, and needs space, so they kick you out if you're sitting in their way, but not before asking you to take a block of cigarettes in your bag for them.

And the customs officers walk through, first ours, and then theirs: ours look a bit old-fashioned compared to theirs, a bit Soviet, the men look meaner and shiftier and the women more dyed blonde and with higher heels; their guys look a bit more dull, bureaucratic, and the women too; and they all know, and the women know they know, and it goes on, again and again, a ritual dance to mark the territory where the land of freedom begins and the land of drudgery ends, back and forth, every day, they do their dance, keeping the gods of the borders happy with their meagre offerings, the glum priests in their uniforms and hats officiating.

And then it's Schengen. But inside Schengen it's not quite true to say that there are no borders. The borders do exist, for some of us. Like on the way here, when we were driving through Germany, some place not far from Berlin, some little town, they stopped us. Why? Ukrainian plates of course. Got a little EU flag on your number plate? No problem: drive back and forth for the rest of your life from Gdańsk to Gibraltar, knock yourself out. But a poor little Ukrainian flag and our funny little dirty number plates: sorry, we just remembered we have a German border that needs protecting. Because Ukrainian number plates don't just drive through Germany just like that. Ukrainian number plates don't just go on holiday along the autobahns, not just like that.

This German stops us, a little guy, not like a German, and you could see that he knew something was up, just by looking at us. They took us off for questioning, and checked our documents, and the guy who was driving us disappeared somehow. The others had Belgian visas, and only my papers weren't good for Germany apparently, only for Poland. Then questioning, with an interpreter, then into a cell, then questioning again, then into a different cell. Who are you, where are you from, where are you going, why? And this lasted the whole day, and overnight, and the next day: and then they tell me I'm being deported.

But then the interpreter, God bless him, a neat little guy from western Ukraine somewhere, you could see he was trying to help, I think he felt sorry for me, maybe he saw his little sister in me or something, he tells me that I have a choice of how to get kicked out of Germany: either they deport you, and you get a big DEPORTED stamped in your passport, or, if you have the cash, you buy yourself a ticket, and your Polish visa gets ANNULLED stamped on it. He said go for the latter option. Well, who wouldn't rather be annulled than deported? They took me into town, bought me plane tickets with my money, and they say off you go, your flight's tomorrow, here's a piece of paper, give it to them when you get on the plane to prove you've left the country. Want to stay another night in our cells before you go? No, thanks.

That's how the border catches you. Because the border isn't just a place: the border is inside you. You have the border stamped on your face, in your passport, on your number plates, it's encoded into your obscure language, always there when you speak, like a wrong harmony in a song, and a little German will always be there to hear it, to read it, and to stamp it on you again to make sure it doesn't fade. And even when you cross the real border, there's a part of you that's still on the other side, part of you that just can't step across. And once you've made the decision to cross, you're split for ever in two, and there's always a bit of you that never left, that is stuck there, afraid to join the rest of you on the right side of the line, because it feels like a traitor, because it feels like a criminal, taking something that doesn't belong to it.

No, thanks, I said, and went off into Berlin. Berlin is all blocks and roads and rails and infrastructure and grey, it felt like it was just pretending to be Western Europe, pretending to be something it wasn't, just like I was. Maybe that little feeling of being at home in Berlin was what made me decide not to take the plane. Maybe the fact that I'd come this far already and they'd just let me out, just like that, after those cells and all the questioning: it felt like a reprieve, like they were almost saying, okay, we did our bit, we ticked our box and filled in our form, now it's up to you. And it felt stupid to go home.

Schengen, of course, has another end, another border. And if you thought it was hard getting in the Polish end, try getting out the French end into Britain. Britain does borders well. It comes naturally, I guess. It's not by accident that there's a big chunk of sea in the way, a moat around the castle. There isn't even a drawbridge, though I suppose there is an underground tunnel you can try to crawl through. And those ferries: like crossing the Styx. I had to pay my boatman too. My boatman was a Lithuanian who got me a very expensive Lithuanian ID card. It wasn't what I had been expecting. They had taken my money and told me they'd sort out my documents. What that meant, I didn't know, and they wouldn't have told me if I'd asked. And I didn't want to ask.

I got to Dover on the boat, with my new document, which did look quite like me: my document, which wasn't mine. In Dover I told them:

it's me, it's me. And they said it's not you, it's not you. I almost believed myself. Okay, the details on the card are not exactly mine, but the main thing is that I am here in front of you and I am me, and I have this card, which is real: I'm no worse than whoever that is. She's at home in Lithuania and not here, so you can let me in in her place, right, what's the difference?

But no. Not you, not you. They had a good rummage through my stuff looking for another ID, the real one for the real me, right through all my clothes, they even had a good laugh at a pair of stupid high-heeled pink sandals that I'd packed, passed them around, marvelled at our exotic Ukrainian fashions. And then straight back on the ferry, with some guy to hand me over to the police in France. The sea was calm: it was the border that made me sick. The guards, the explaining, the searching, trying to believe for a second that it's really me on that card because if I really believe, they might let me in, if only I can be someone else convincingly enough.

The French cells were definitely not as nice as the German ones: small with this horrible toilet in the corner. And more questions, and more police, and this time the interpreter also wanted to help me. He offered to get me out of this mess if I slept with him. He said it right there in front of the police, knowing they couldn't understand. At least you can always rely on your countrymen to step in and help you in your hour of need, those knights in shining armour, real Cossack heroes. I wasn't having it, of course. And after a couple of days of questioning, I was off to a detention centre. Now I was really, properly locked up. In Europe's bin, with all the other rubbish.

And then, like some kind of bad joke, after a week they did the same thing, they let me go. They kept my Lithuanian ID, gave me a piece of paper and told me to get out of France. This was now my only document. At that moment, that's who I was: Get Out Of France. One of the people there, a woman, offered me a lift into the next town. I said no, no thanks. I just wanted to get out of there and away from them and just be on my own and free to move, to walk that way or this, run around, lie down in a field or whatever, I couldn't even bear to sit in a car with them for ten minutes. And so I walked like an idiot along this busy road not even knowing where the town was and eventually met some people with bikes who couldn't speak English and I five words of French, but they pointed me in the right direction.

I managed to contact my Lithuanian, and he came up with a new plan and a new document. He said go on this other, long ferry by some islands, British islands near France, where they don't check too carefully, and then you get to a place called Poole and then you go to London. Why didn't you tell me this the first time? Obviously the stupid amount of money he took for his ID card the first time didn't stretch to this new information about this Poole. So I went on that ferry, by those islands, and they came on and the guy sits down next to me and asks me where I'm going, and why, and why I'm on my own, and so on, and he doesn't like the new ID too much. I'll come back to you, he says.

And here some miracle happened. He didn't come back. The boat was only in that port for a little while and they had a lot of people to go round, and there was a lot of commotion, and whatever happened, I don't know, but he didn't get back to me, and there I stayed, and I got to Poole.

I got to Poole with twenty euros, and I knew that wouldn't get me to London. But I walked to the bus station anyway. And here was the second miracle. I asked the bus driver how much the ticket to London cost, and said I only had twenty euros. He laughed, and said he'd take me for nothing: it was the middle of the night and he was driving an almost empty bus. I was so grateful to that driver, I don't think he realised.

And in London I got in touch with a family friend who helped me find a room in a place with the beautiful English name Manor House. It was not the kind of place the name suggested. The room was in a cramped flat being sublet by a family of Bulgarians, who for some reason spoke bad Polish to me. And then I was immediately chewed by bedbugs. I'd never encountered a bedbug until England. Then the family friend got me my first job, and that was it: I started cleaning London. And London was very dirty. It wasn't quite what I had been expecting, after negotiating all the Polish and German and French and English border guards and the creepy interpreter, after two jails and a detention centre. Where was London? Where was the Manor House?

So we've been driving north and north for hours now, and the sky is getting colder and bigger and darker, and I say to O., so when are we getting to this border? I can't take the tension already, when will they check us? And she just looks at me as though I've asked her if she is sure the world isn't flat, and says under her raised eyebrow, my dear, we crossed the border ages ago, you're in Scotland already and no one is going to check anything.

This really is something new, I think: a border with no guards, no dogs, no bribes, no detention centre, no jail, where nobody goes through your underwear, nobody wants to sleep with you, nobody locks you up, nobody says its not you, not you. This really is something new, I think. And somehow I don't feel so sick any more.

Sheena Blackhall

DYEUK'S DOWP
*A Scots owersett of 'Drakestail', a classic French fairy tale published
by Charles Marelle in 1888 under the title 'Bout-d'-Canard' in*
Affenschwanz et Cetera

Aince there wis a byordnar wee dyeuk wi an unca loud quack. Sae they
caad him Quacklin.

Noo, Quacklin wis gleg an he vrocht hard, sae he saved up a rowth
o siller. In fack, he saved up sae muckle that the King hissel cam tae
borra frae the dyeuk.

Quacklin wis prood tae len his siller tae the King. Bit a year gaed by,
syne twa, syne three, an the King niver pyed him back.

'I've wyted lang eneuch,' quo Quacklin. Sae he tuik a pyoke for the
siller, an he sterted for the castle, skreichin, 'Quack! Quack! Quack! I
wint ma siller back!'

Afore lang, he cam upon a Laidder leanin teetle a waa.

'Whaur are ye gaun, Quacklin?' speired Laidder.

'Tae the King for ma siller,' quo Quacklin.

'Tae the King!' cried Laidder. 'Thon's winnerfu! Will ye takk me
wi ye?'

'Why nae?' speired Quacklin. 'A body can niver hae ower mony friens.'
An he skreiched oot, 'Quack! Quack! Quack! Laidder inno pyoke!'

Faist as a glisk, Laidder wis in the pyoke. Syne Quacklin traivelled
on, cryin, 'Quack! Quack! Quack! I wint my siller back!'

A wee whylie eftir, he cam upon a Burnie rinnin ben a wid.

'Whaur are ye gaun, Quacklin?' speired the Burnie.

'Tae the King for ma siller,' quo Quacklin.

'Tae the King!' cried the Burnie. 'Thon's winnerfu! Will ye takk me
wi ye?'

'Why nae?' speired Quacklin. 'A body can niver hae ower mony friens.'
And he skreiched oot, 'Quack! Quack! Quack! Burnie inno pyoke!'

Faist as a glisk, Burnie wis in the pyoke. Syne Quacklin traivelled
on, cryin, 'Quack! Quack! Quack! I wint my siller back!'

A wee whylie eftir, he cam upon a Beeskepp hingin frae a tree.

'Whaur are ye gaun, Quacklin?' speired the Beeskepp.

'Tae the King for ma siller,' quo Quacklin.

'Tae the King!' cried the Beeskepp. 'Thon's winnerfu! Will ye takk me wi ye?'

Noo Quacklin's pyoke wis growin rale wechty, bit he thocht the Beeskepp micht fit.

'Why nae?' speired Quacklin. 'A body can niver hae ower mony friens.' And he skreiched oot, 'Quack! Quack! Quack! Beeskepp inno pyoke!'

Faist as a glisk, Beeskepp wis in the pyoke.

Syne Quacklin traivelled on, cryin, 'Quack! Quack! Quack! I wint my siller back!'

Sune eftir, Quacklin cam tae the King's castle. He merched right up tae the guairds an telt them, 'I'm here for ma siller!'

The guairds gaed inbye an telt the Prime Minister. The Prime Minister telt the King.

'Wha dis thon Quacklin think he is?' speired the King. 'Niver mind. Jist fling him doon the pit!'

Sae they flang Quacklin doon the pit an left him thonner.

'Help!' skreiched Quacklin. 'I'll niver get oot!'

Syne he myndit on the Laidder. Sae he skirled oot, 'Quack! Quack! Quack! Laidder oot o pyoke.'

Faist as a glisk, Laidder wis oot o the pyoke. Laidder leaned teetle the side o the pit, an Quacklin sclimmed oot.

Syne Quacklin stude there, skreichin, 'Quack! Quack! Quack! I wint ma siller back!'

'Hou did thon Quacklin win oot o the pit?' winnered the King. 'Niver mind. Jist pit him in the pottie.'

Sae they pit Quacklin in the pottie an set it on the lowe.

'Help!' cried Quacklin. 'I'm bein byled for denner!'

Syne he myndit Burnie. Sae he skelloched oot, 'Quack Quack! Quack! Burnie oot o pyoke!'

Faist as a glisk, Burnie wis oot o the pyoke. Burnie pit oot the lowe an ran awa.

Syne Quacklin got oot, skirlin, 'Quack Quack! Quack! I wint ma siller back!'

'Quacklin's oot o the pottie!' raged the King. 'Niver mind. Jist bring him here, an I'll sattle him – for guid!'

Sae they brocht Quacklin tae the King. The King ettled tae grab him. 'Help!' skreiched Quacklin. 'This is the eyn!'

Syne he myndit on Beeskepp. Sae he skelloched oot, 'Quack! Quack! Quack! Beeskepp oot o pyoke!'

Faist as a glisk, Beeskepp wis oot o the pyoke. The bees heezed frae the skepp an sterted tae sting the King.

'Help!' skirled the King. He fled frae the castle, an the bees follaed. They chased him aa the wey tae the Back o Beyond, an he wis niver seen again.

'Hooray!' skirled the fowk o the castle, an the Prime Minister quo, 'We niver likit thon King onywey.'

Sae they pit Quacklin on the throne an gied him a croon.

'Will ye be oor King?' speired the guairds.

'Why nae?' quo Quacklin. 'A body can niver hae ower mony friens.'

Tom Bryan

EXCEPT YOU, SON

December. Snowing. It's 4.30 p.m. and the Post Office closes at 5. There are three counters. There are maybe fifteen people in the queue. Many have parcels for posting so the queue is moving slowly . . . but it is moving. There is tinsel on the walls framing posters giving last posting dates to America, Canada, New Zealand or Australia.

'Ah'm nae bad ken.'

'Need tae get these parcels aff tae Australia. My granddaughter's there. It'll no be snowin' there. Aye, it's summer Down Under.'

'Summer? Whit's that?'

Then, *she* breenges in like a polar bear. A big woman. Tracksuit bottoms, trainers. A black short-sleeve t-shirt that says FECK in red letters. No winter coat or hat.

Sometimes in music, a note or chord changes. From major to minor, happy to sad, quick to slow. The note in the post office had changed. It reminds me of the old silent films where the Canadian Mountie or fur trapper enters the log cabin while the blizzard rages outside. The door slams shut and with it the cold and wind: 'Not a fit night out for man nor beast,' he usually says.

She takes her place at the end of the queue. We all wait. The light talking has stopped. She is smoking until someone reminds her it is not allowed.

'Nae problem.' She stubs it out on a table then bins it. 'Can this queue no speed up? Ah'v messages tae git.'

No reply, though one clerk at the counter looks up, in the general direction.

I am ahead of her in the queue but like a nervous driver who is being tailgated, I am aware that she is back there somewhere. There is now a collective silent wish for the queue to move more quickly, for her sake, for all our sakes.

FECK is now shuffling from one big foot to the other, and making a snorting noise, a kind of nasal *harrumph, harrumph, harrumph.*

'Sorry bit ah'm in a hurry. Ye'll no mind if I dae some queue jumpin?'
Without waiting for an answer, she shuffles around our left and
almost skids to the front of the queue on the wet floor.

Some protest:

'Wait yer turn . . .'

'Who dae ye think ye are? Haud yer horses.'

'Whit's the hurry?'

The man at the front of the queue is body-shunted aside but behind
her back he makes a crazy circle with his finger at the side of his
head. *She is mental. Leave her be. Let her go. The sooner she's seen to
the quicker she leaves.* Unspoken but we all understand. Our body
language says we all agree.

She is at the counter now. 'Ah'm needin mah car tax.'

'Do you have a certificate of insurance and a valid MOT?'

'Jist had the MOT done.'

'I'm sorry, miss, but you need to produce a valid certificate of insurance and your most recent MOT certificate.'

'Whit's this then?'

Like flying a paper plane, she floats a certificate across the counter.

'This is only your car tax request for payment.'

'Aye, and here's the money.' She slides the cash under the barrier.

'I'm sorry but we also need to see the other documents . . .'

'Other documents mah arse. Is mah cash no good enough for ye?
Snobs. Ye're aw snobs.' She grabs the cash back and stuffs it in her
tracksuit pocket.

She turns to the queue. We look to our feet. Shuffle nervously. A few
people further back in the queue leave for the door. I think to myself:
She's gonna blow I think, she's gonna blow.

Then just as that musical note changed when she came in, it
changes again.

She speaks in a low voice, with her chin to her chest. It is a soft voice,
almost like a child's.

'Aye, ah sometimes jist wish ah wiz a bird.'

Some smile at this. This huge woman in a tracksuit and trainers,
turning into a small bird.

She reads our minds. 'Aye, even a totie wee bird wid be jist fine. Jist fine.'

She now looms over the queue of only about six people. We can't leave now. We have to see this thing through. One counter clerk disappears into the office, making a phone motion with her pinkie and thumb. We read her lips. *I'm going to phone the police.*

'Aye, even a wee bird would be fine. Coz . . . coz . . . listen up aabody . . . I'd fly up tae the ceiling then . . . then . . .

'*Shite doon on the whole lot of youse!*'

Whirling, she points to the counter. '*And youse as well.*' I am possibly smiling but also nervous, looking down at my wet shoes. But it is over. She turns for the door.

She is going. Thank God she is going.

Hell, I jump.

She's come back!

She's gripped my left shoulder.

Hard.

Then her grip turns to an open hand. She pats me twice on the shoulder.

'Except you, son. *You're* awright.'

Someone sniggers. Then the whole post office bursts into laughter.

Later, I see her plodding home up the long hill. The streetlight magnifies the heavy snow. With her bare arms and t-shirt, she seems tiny and lonesome against the dark winter hills in the distance. She seems smaller than any bird.

Jim Carruth

RHINO IN THE ROOM

A rhinoceros in the room
is a different case entirely

never happier than being
talked about constantly

a party's biggest splash
to an audience of ripples;

a serial mingler he works
the cliques in every room.

And that trick he does with
the salmon mousse canapés

piercing them with his horn
to create a little pink halo.

The other ploy he often uses
that angry snort head down

just to see their arms wave,
his name on everyone's lips.

Andrew Cattanach

PLAYTIME

I liked it when Susie would come round. Her mother and my mother would be angry in the kitchen and me and Susie would be in the living room and she'd be spitting Robinson's into my mouth. Sometimes we played at tongue-touchers and even one time she licked my eye. Father would be there from time to time and if he was in the mood he'd be talking whispers at himself.

Did you hear that? he'd say.

And I'd be like, No.

And all the time Susie would be minding her own business, not listening to nothing.

*

When we were a smidge older, Father would come into the living room where me and Susie would be watching kids' stuff.

What's that smell? he'd say, a look of pure disgust on his big face. There's a right tang about the place, isn't that so, Susie? And then he'd wink and walk away as if the atmosphere was too much to bear.

I always thought it him saying something about me being in the sweaty part of life. Susie would go a ripe red colour every time he did it, too, which made me think he and her had some joke together. I hated that – as if they were having a right old giggle at my expense but with Susie too kind to let on.

It was only when I was bigger and my sister Belle was getting bigger too that I worked out what was smelling so bad.

*

Have you shagged her yet? Father asked me one time. We were in the living room and he was watching the snooker.

Susie, he said. Have you shagged her?

I couldn't look at him for my hot face. Just kept pushing the truck through the carpet pile.

He laughed.

You're just a wee boy, he said. A wee boy that plays with toys all day and wrestles with his winky-dink at night. And he said it in a way that meant I'd never be anything else, that I'd always be alone in the dark and never shagging no one.

*

You should see Susie now, all big and fat and nothing more of her old Rich Tea hair. Folk laugh about her all the time; say she would shag a leper colony if only they asked nicely. For a while, Father would carry around a pair of her knick-knacks for showing people and having a laugh. He'd take them out of his pocket, slowly, like a clown or something. And there they'd be – really big but kind of skimpy too – like a long line of lace, and you didn't know which bit went where but you knew they were XXL.

Mother hated it when he would show her Big Fat Susie's knick-knacks. We'd be eating and Father would get them out under the table, just to be a menace, and we'd have a giggle. Mother would pretend there was nothing there. But then she'd get up for a bit of butter or something and when she turned back, there in her beans would be Big Fat Susie's smalls. I couldn't help it but laugh. Mother, though, was anything but on the laughing side of things when it came to those big pants.

*

One time, when the day was full up of heat, Big Fat Susie came chapping on the door carrying a babe in her arms, and before anyone could say a word Mother had chucked a fist right on Susie's horrible snout and slammed the door on her face. I'd never seen Mother so mad. She had a right rage on her that day.

Father was home later that night. He had heard all about Big Fat Susie's bloody trough plough and he looked dark and sombre, thinking he'd probably have to say sorry and that he loved Mother. And when we sat down for dinner there was this grim silence and the kitchen felt hot and then cold like it was going to rain. It was horrible-silent. But then all of a sudden Mother just burst. It was like nothing I'd seen before. She couldn't stop giggling. And then Father too. And then I joined in, all of us having a right old wheeze at Big Fat Susie getting popped in the face by Mother. Right funny.

Don't see her much any more, Susie. She lives over the way now. Just her and her army of babes. Mother thought it would be over between her and Susie's mother, what with punching her daughter and all. But Susie's mother said that the fat cow had it coming. Would have lamped her one herself if she wasn't beat to it.

Daughter or no, Susie's mother said, you can't go around like that and not expect a thump.

But Mother reckoned she was all talk and wouldn't harm an insect really. As wet as piss, she said.

I'll lie in bed sometimes and think about Susie's place over the way; the messy house with the great crowd of babes, their hands full of biscuits and their cups brimming with juice. All those hours of winky-dink in the dark. And it's like the living-room tumbles all over again; her mother and my mother talking shouts in the kitchen, golden hair against my face and the burn of Robinson's on the throat. Your eyes back then were a pale blue, your tongue a sweet-soft thing against mine.

Regi Claire

AS IF IT WERE A GAME

I am spinning again. Spinning the threads that one day soon will make up the tapestry of House. Black and blue threads, red and green, yellow, purple and pink. The cats are asleep at last, even the three kittens in the bottom drawer of my worktable. There's no air today, not the flimsiest flitter of a current, despite the dormer windows being mouths agape. My neighbours always misunderstand. Deliberately misunderstand when I tell them how it is and has to be. How it can't be. Mustn't be. That boy downstairs, for example. He needs taught a lesson. Why is it that children have become masters and despots, wicked little wielders of power? Why have parents become fearful of them? Take Frau Meyer. Soft as a ripe peach. Round and downy and flushed. Squashable. Her little girls have already learnt that she can be plucked and swallowed whole, stone and all. But boys and girls need to be smacked, especially boys like Matthias. And so, one day soon, my red and pink and purple threads will join together and, interwoven, form a pattern that will run in one thrumming glister all the way through the tapestry of House.

*

The neighbours' brats had been hollering and squealing in the garden all afternoon, so loudly Bambino started to growl and Dino had to slam shut the balcony door. God, how he hated the little buggers. Why couldn't they go and play elsewhere? All he wanted just now was to enjoy his cup of jasmine infusion, the aroma wafting up into his face in fragrant curls of steam. His mobile tinkled. 'Tonight?' the message read. 'You game?' The tea had misted his cheeks and he dabbed at them with an Egyptian-cotton handkerchief. He'd always insisted on proper cloth handkerchiefs, ironed for him by his cleaning lady. At the age of thirty-seven, Dino knew the meaning of style. Real style. Not bullshit bogus fakery. Okay, that was larding it on a bit. But it was how he usually talked to the others.

He texted back a smiley, then sipped the tea with his eyes closed, feeling it sun-dapple the inside of his mouth and trickle down his throat in a shower of white blossom. Bambino lay soft as a rug across his knees. Finally Dino glanced at his watch. Five-fifteen, *merda*. He'd need to get his skates on. He wasn't keen on the night shift, but, hey, we all have to scrape a living somehow. And there'd be that little escapade – tomfoolery rather, a cautionary shot across certain people's bows – during his break. Something to look forward to. First, though, a quick dog walk. '*Andiamo!*' He slid the poodle off his lap and went into the kitchen, tipped a tin of sardines and some leftover spaghetti carbonara into the food bowl, then held it under Bambino's nose to remind him dinner was ready and waiting and so, *presto-presto,* round the block and forget the sniffing and surplus squirts. White linen jacket, dog lead, canvas shoes. The hand-stitched Italian loafers wrapped in suede cloth were for later, their thin leather soles perfect for driving, dancing and, if required, some gigolo-ing.

*

When she went into the bathroom, Sabina knew there would be blood. Lots of it. Not for the first time either but, as far as she was concerned, for the last. No more miscarriages from now on and no more babies. She would clamp her legs together until Sigi agreed to use a condom, or else she'd get her tubes snipped in secret.

Her two tireless daughters were playing in the garden with their friend from upstairs. Tiny Tina and not-so-tiny Dora, four and five, with enough lip on them to comfortably out-scream and out-talk her and possibly even Sigi, in the near future. They'd wheedled her into giving them juice, crisps and cake, plus a few old bedsheets and clothes pegs for making a 'tent-house' under the trees. All very domestic, nice and quiet. Or so she'd pictured it. But crouching on the toilet, sweating and rag-doll limp, a slick of empty skin, she could hear their high-pitched yells and the herd-trample of their feet, now on the gravel, now on the grass, as they chased each other round and round and round the house, trapping it in an ever-tighter coil of noise.

Back in the kitchen, she drank two glasses of lukewarm water, then a mug of strong, sugary coffee to get her pulse rocking 'n' rolling. The small TV on the sideboard was spewing late-afternoon drivel. But she couldn't couldn't couldn't get that earlier news item out of her head. The image of a Syrian refugee boy lying face-down on a Mediterranean beach. Just a little kid. Dressed in summer clothes, ready to skip and run along the shore, perhaps in pursuit of a candy-striped ball or a yellow dog. Ready to career straight into the outspread arms of his father, who would hold him fast, for ever and ever.

Children, she kept thinking, all the children slipping into the water without fuss or struggle. Like fish in the ocean they were, shoals of them, but soundless, unmoving, their silvery limbs already turning grey . . .

The phone started ringing as she sat with her eyes wet and helpless. She got to her feet slowly, feeling sluggish and too-heavy, as if parts of her were still carrying the burden of another's life.

*

Hannes rolled over on the sofa and pushed the young woman's breasts out of the way. They were big all right, real 'knockers' – one of the many words his mother had objected to. The memory of her made him shrivel almost instantly. But the girl didn't seem worried. Her breath hot against his shoulder, she'd begun to slide her thighs along his flank, up and down, up and down, stealthily coating him in her wetness. She resembled an overgrown Bambi, doe-eyed, soft and gold-furred as though she hadn't quite shed her teenage skin. Not that she was a teenager any more, God forbid. Just a medical student needing to pay her bills. Her 'ad', if it could be termed that, had been irresistible. A short clip which included a close-up, a knickerless selfie with her fingers darting in and out between her legs as, to all intents and purposes, she sat, dressed in a polka-dot summer frock, taking notes in a lecture theatre full of fellow medics.

Hannes became aware of shouts outside; shadows swept across the curtains as the neighbours' kids stampeded past. He felt faint all of a sudden. Nauseated. What on earth was he doing on his girlfriend's sofa, getting his rocks off with a first-year playing at being a whore? 'Let's stop this charade,' he said, sounding callous even to himself. He wrestled his body into a sitting position, grabbed his t-shirt off the floor to cover his futile erection and, avoiding her stare, scrambled into his jockeys and cut-off jeans. Then he dug into his pocket for a handful of notes. 'That cover your efforts?'

The girl shrugged. 'Whatever.' She looked sullen, offended. He'd hurt her pride. The pride of a high achiever who liked to succeed in any line of business. Well, he certainly hoped she wouldn't become a surgeon or, if she did, that he'd never end up under her knife.

*

Cleo touched her upper lip. Still numb and swollen. Gingerly she fitted a glass of lemonade between her teeth and took a sip.

'What's wrong, Mummy?' Matthias, who had rushed indoors as soon as she'd arrived home, was regarding her with the suspicion of a child in constant fear of losing his only parent, the one person who stood between him and a strange and hostile world.

'I'll be fine once the dentist's injection has worn off.' Her smile felt lopsided.

'Worn off?'

'Going away, going . . . going . . . gone!' And she slapped him lightly on the seat of his shorts, damp from all his dashing about.

He grimaced, then sidled over to the food cupboard where he helped himself to a jam doughnut. Barely five years old and already . . . Well, she didn't care. She watched him silently as he wolfed it down. He was licking the sugar off his fingers when the doorbell rang. Oh shit, not now – not with her mouth all crooked like it had been wasp-stung or sucked by a crazy lover.

Out on the landing stood the cat-loving hag from the top floor. Again. A twist of multicoloured threads trailed from her hands like she'd had her wires ripped out.

Hiding her smirk behind a tissue, Cleo lisped, 'Oh, hello, Frau Roth. Been to the dentist . . .'

Frau Roth, with a dismissive gesture at Matthias, barked in her hard-of-hearing way, 'Your boy!' Then she slitted her eyes. 'I saw him. Running around the garden he was with his . . . his *thingy* hanging out and the girls from downstairs right behind him. *Snatching* at it and *giggling* as

if it were a game. Don't you know you need to *break* a child? *Break* him
and *break* him, until he learns how to behave?' And off she stomped,
nodding her white scraggle-head, back to her tapestries and her cat
menagerie under the eaves.

'I'm sorry,' Cleo cried after her. 'Frau Meyer was supposed to keep
an eye on him.' Then her shoulders began to shake with laughter. But,
dammit, she shouldn't have dropped Sabina into this.

Matthias had slunk off to his room. 'Son?' She put her head round
the door, held the tissue to her mouth so he wouldn't see her grin.
'No more willy games, all right? Or Frau Roth will make sure you won't
be allowed to play with Dora and Tina any more.' He didn't look up
from his tablet.

Need a man in the house, she told herself as she slid down onto the
couch and reached for her cigarettes. Puffing away a little clumsily
because of the numbness, she pictured Kathi's new boyfriend downstairs.
A bit young, maybe, but a real stud of a guy. Around at odd hours
and not always alone, it seemed. And not with Kathi either, whose
environmentalist job clearly took her abroad too often for a full-blooded
male like him. Earlier today when crossing the lawn to tell Matthias
she was off to the dentist's, Cleo had passed Kathi's patio where the
man was seated at his computer, tanned legs propped sideways on a
chair, headphones over his ears to block out the kids. His eyes had met
hers, probing, liquid and hot, and she'd become conscious of the sun
at her back and the thinness of her dress.

Cleo cupped one of her breasts in her free hand, then gave it a gentle
squeeze. Firm and ripe for the picking. She smiled a lazy smile. Later
this evening, once Matthias was asleep, she would slip downstairs with
a bottle of wine to welcome the young man to the house. Her lip was
beginning to tingle. By tonight she'd be able to blow smoke rings again,
and all sensation would have returned.

*

Dino peered into the glove compartment to check on the gun. It was
a replica, of course, but looked real enough. So real, in fact, that he'd
shrunk away when Reto had pointed it at him in the toilet of the

taxi company where they both worked. He was parked under a large chestnut tree up on Cemetery Hill, his windows down to let in the leafy coolness. The air tasted of metal. Storm clouds were stacked up like phantom fortresses. As he stared through the windscreen smeared with dead insects, the battlements erupted in white zigzags of light that fractured the sky and stabbed at the wooded ridge on the far side of the valley. Dino felt his eyes waver, then refocus. Thunder rumbled in the distance like an afterthought. He put on his Ray-Bans, but there was no sun now, only a lurid bruise slowly getting overlaid by the murk of darkness. There would be no rain either, not tonight. He sat for a moment longer. The cemetery chapel's clock dinged the hour. Did the mourners ever notice how childishly shrill it sounded, almost cheerful, as they dragged their sorrow and watering cans along the gravel paths? The bell fell silent and the echo rippled out into the heavy stillness of an evening that smelt of lilies, roses and cut grass, of damp moss and the earthy odour of ivy torn off a wall, and a small plot of land freshly turned. *Basta*, he thought almost angrily before restarting the engine.

The dispatcher's voice came over the radio while he was stuck at a red light. 'Get your ass down to the railway station, Dino. Fares needing rides and all the other drivers are busy.' Sheet lightning fizzled out beyond the hills and Dino wished the dispatcher flash-fried into oblivion. Wished it for just an instant, because he rather liked the man and his rough banter.

Waiting at the head of the short queue was Sigi, his downstairs neighbour, body almost bursting out of his clothes as if he couldn't wait to get home and get it on with his butterball of a wife. Dino grinned as he leaned over to depress the door handle.

But Sigi looked pale, and his fleshiness sagged. 'What's up?' Dino asked.

Sigi sighed. 'It's my mother. Had another fall at the care home and now, well . . .' He shrugged, lowered his head. 'I have to fetch Sabina. Might be the last time we—'

Dino drove. Bambino would be ecstatic to see him, if only for a second. Delicately, Dino operated the pedals, braked and accelerated with feeling, his feet in the thin-soled Italian shoes vibrating as they danced to a rhythm all their own.

*

Sabina was ready when she heard the taxi stop outside. She'd changed from her sweat-stained shorts into a flouncy summer dress and sandals, then deposited Dora and Tina, together with some leftover cake, at Cleo's. Cleo had mentioned Frau Roth's complaint, saying she hoped Matthias hadn't upset the girls? Her son was due for a small procedure at the hospital next week to help him pee more easily. Which was why he was a little obsessed with his willy right now. 'Fingers crossed he'll grow out of it, more or less . . .' And she'd winked. Sabina had tried not to wince.

Now she almost collided with Dino as he ran up the stairs 'to say hello to Bambino'. Her husband was sitting slumped in the taxi. He didn't even raise his head when she got in the back, merely muttered, 'God, I'm exhausted.' Sabina felt like replying, *So am I*, but bit her tongue. Through the window she caught sight of a quiver of lightning that seemed briefly to illuminate the house. No thunder followed; the storm had moved off towards the lake.

She thought of the refugee families again – all those grandparents, parents and children fleeing from place to place, country to country, without respite, without houses to feel safe in, without care homes to look after their dying . . .

*

House, meanwhile, near-strangled by the noise and shouts it has endured all afternoon, all summer in fact, decides to play a game of its own. It has grown accustomed to people *listening* as they lie sleepless in the dark, skewered by their restless minds despite closed eyes and relaxation exercises – listening to its sighs and occasional deliberate groans, its windy whines and gurglings, its creaks, sudden sharp snaps and the rustlings of the small creatures that inhabit or, according to some, infest its hollow spaces. But now that night has fallen and the stars are out in a clear, empty sky, House will become a listener itself and listen to *them*. Of the consequences it doesn't, or can't, think. So what if someone talks in their sleep? House can do nothing. Or can it? Start a fire, maybe, or burst a pipe? Release an army of ants or woodlice? And what about that wasps' nest tucked between the corner roof beams, could House make it crack to let its inmates swarm and sting?

The first hour is unremarkable because half the people are still out and about. Only the clatter of the computer keyboard on the ground floor; muzak on the floor above. The usual whiffles and snuffles of the old woman and the children (all safely in bed now, the little girls monitored by the single woman until their parents' return) and of that tiresome dog, whose sharp teeth have so often ravaged House's skirting, and the equally tiresome cats with their claws that scratch and gouge its walls as they scramble to the tops of doors to drape themselves into draught excluders.

The next few hours are alive with activity, as though the day's events have lit a fuse. Footsteps. Doors opening and closing. The ground-floor parquet beginning to squeak under a bucking bed and, later, a sofa. But the cries are too muffled. Only the cats below the eaves scream a little louder. More footsteps, more doors.

House, of course, can do much better. And so it does. Indulges in a series of rapid cracks that vibrate through its skeleton as it relieves itself of the built-up heat and tension.

Just before dawn, House hears someone talk in their sleep. '*Merda,*' the voice is saying. Then again, '*Merda.*' After a garbled few words: 'Only a replica, Dino. To warn them off. We're people too. Live and let live. Or else, hit back. Hit hard.' Garble-garble-garble. Whimpers. 'Didn't mean to hurt anyone. Wouldn't hurt a fly.' Mewling. Could be the dog, whose unclipped nails now scratch at the bedroom door.

House has had enough. Rattling its bones, it heaves its ribcage so the door springs open and the dog scuttles over to the bed, jumps on the coverlet and begins to paw at the man's face. The man screams, lashes out. The dog yelps. Someone starts to knock on a door.

'Dino? Dino? You okay?' It's the single woman, whose smoking habit has clogged up House's vents for years. She is wearing a kimono, and her skin is still flushed from her earlier exploits downstairs.

House shivers itself just enough to slam the woman's door shut, *bang*, locking her out, if only temporarily. She will be forced to ring her bell now and wake the boy.

In the end the commotion wakes them all; the whole sorry houseful are assembled on the first-floor landing, except for the cat woman under the eaves, who refuses to wear hearing aids. But she belongs to House anyway. Has long ago become its human agent and will soon, once she has served her purpose, be reabsorbed into the timber and brickwork. The children have started to slide down the banisters and House considers another shake, then contents itself with a wobble that makes the younger girl scream.

'A nightmare,' the man called Dino says, 'just a nightmare.'

The young man from the ground floor sneaks off as soon as possible, all done in, after a hungry glance at the woman in the kimono. His musky smell fills the stairwell. Come lunchtime, he will log into that website again, skip from image to video clip to image, then make his choice.

The couple with the two small girls is more discreet. Older. But the man's hand fumbles for the woman's all the same and his large body folds and leans into her as if he hasn't got the strength to support himself. As if his power has been switched off at source. Will he ever recover his fleshy fervour? Will he find solace in the arms of a certain trainee medic, perhaps, who combines her night shifts at the local care home with a more personal, more lucrative service for the nearly or newly bereft?

That leaves the man called Dino and the woman in the kimono with the boy. 'Back to bed,' she murmurs as she huddles over the child, stroking his head. She smiles at the man, 'And no more nightmares,' then closes her door. Having put the boy to bed, she will go and sit on the couch, light a cigarette and then another, and another as she contemplates her future, her gaze fixed on the still-bright morning star. Will she see it? Or will she be waiting for the sun, the sun and its scorching ways?

The man stands alone for a moment, the dog keeping its distance, tail between legs. In time they will come to trust each other again. The man will forget about his nightmare, almost. He will remind himself that it was only a replica gun and didn't do much harm. Not too much, at any rate.

House has learnt a great deal from tonight's experience and hopes to develop its skills. For the present, though, as the sun rises red and fiery in the east to stoke up another day to furnace temperatures, House allows itself to drowse a little, safe in the knowledge that come nightfall it will play another game with its guests. Because that's what they really are, aren't they, its guests. Only its guests. And there are all sorts of things you can do to your guests.

Ken Cockburn

POEM FOR MY FATHER ON HIS
SEVENTY-NINTH BIRTHDAY

He is in the garage.
He is in the warehouse.
He is in the greenhouse.
He is in the garden.

He is on the golf-course.
He is on the stage.
He is on the beach.
He is on the dance-floor.

He wears a dressing gown.
He wears swimming trunks.
He wears blue overalls.
He wears a suit.

He has a hammer.
He has a dishtowel.
He has a briefcase.
He has a trowel.

He is at the Links Market.
He is in Lower Largo.
He is in Harrogate.
He is in Glen Fender.

He is walking the dog.
He is boarding his ship.
He is clearing the table.
He is driving home.

Graham Fulton

SHEEPS

Fresh lambs. Lamb-shaped.
Meat for Man. Fuel for the pot.

White, black, in between.
Staring at air with soft-focus eyes.

Chewing in unison, practising love.
Mounting each other, bouncing around,
wandering through their gentle routines.
Standing, lying, running away,
wondering why

the plural of lamb is lambs,
but the plural of sheep is sheep,
as if it's lost in the growing-
up. The sacrifice of *I* to *We*.

It goes in,
it comes out.

Scatters of dung, shiny, tiny, some
like sculptures by Henry Moore.
Clinkers caught in the mythical fleece,
wondering why their mothers
keep going *baaaa*
in a desperate low-toned voice,
or going *baaaa*
in a high-toned voice.

Sucking the world from a tasty nipple,
all the traits of a happy human.

A timid trickle of milky piddle
melting into the wired-in grass.

Itchy parents rub their rears
on the posts of a metal pasture fence.
Side to side, up and down.
A parasite tango, a fleabag fandango.

Feels so good!
It needs to be done.

Their babies with mental whirring tails.
Metronomes at the speed of sound.

Eager for *being*
but not knowing what *being* is.
Afraid of everything,
but not knowing what anything

is.

Content with one more dawn in the field.
Lying in pairs, cuddling for comfort,
waiting alone, staring at space.
All the traits of a happy human.

A light in your face, at least,
for a while.

Lesley Glaister

HOGWEED

It hogs the verges,
coarse, thick stemmed,
priapic, even its buds are purple fists.

Last night I saw the same type
in the pub, hogging the bar,
pint in fist:

shaved skull, tattoos, scars,
a wide-legged stance
as if his balls were vast.

But when a girl
came close his face
broke open like a bud

and somewhere on a verge
a fist unfurled,
each finger tipped with sparkling lace.

WORLD SERVICE

You leak like conscience
from a plastic bud
drought, torture, hijab
jihad, rape and flood –

strange lullaby. Dreams mix
with drones and planes
and dead fish swimming
in a field of flames.

I lose the bud,
wake snarled in hair
and wires – plug-in oppression
poverty, polluted air,

a baby's cries, a melting glacier.
Hang on your voices through the night
judicious, grown-up, safely far
like parents heard

behind a door. Sheets twisted,
nightdress nightmare sour,
I clutch you to my ear,
to interfere, block out

my own dark noise.

Andrew Greig

KITTLENAKED WOOD

For George Boyter and Mike Heron

Have you seen anything since
    harmless and puzzling
        as the gorgeous black and gold

dressing-gown spread over thorn
    by the edge of Kittlenaked Wood
        that morning so many years ago,

dew-dripping, goat-stinking, inexplicable,
    while its owner, some couthy
        divinity of the back-country,

the Pan of Fife,
    curly-loined, shaggy, dextrous,
        ran wild across the tattie dreels,

the thin skreel of his pipes
    firing pee-wit and gull
        high over Kellie Law?

                    *

Could be we were right,
not so daft as we sat
cross-legged by our fire
in cloaks, tabards, tea-cosy hats,
smoking cinnamon sticks,
blowing moothie, whistle, kazoo,
re-inventing Arcadia
in back-country Fife.

As the cider went down
and the sausages charred,
we knew this much:
the enchanted world
if anywhere
is our backyard.

Laughter and hush
when wind dropped and moon rose
through the peopled wood?
Had it been solemn,
it could not have been true.

                    *

You'll mind how we tracked him
        lit up by nothing stronger
                than cider, mandolins and Baudelaire,

coming through Kittlenaked Wood
        in courtly dusk
                to glimpse our Pan, planted snug

in the fork of a sturdy nyad,
        giggling as sonsie fauns and nymphs
                whooped across dew-clobbered fields,

and from cloven heels
        unanimous and moonlit
                arose glittering the Scottish Verdict:

'*Not Proven*'

*

Fellow conjurors, we were wrong
    or at least misinformed
        only in this

that kept us blissful for a while:
    It's easy. It was not.
        Yet the fearlessness that came (and went)

with being young and daft
    bides in that neglected place
        (cut down and ploughed in years ago),

as grey hairs and dodgy knees
    bear what's left of our hearts and minds
        towards something we never entirely forsook

('*Heave a stretch and sigh a yawn*
    hark now life has just begun')
        in the heart of Kittlenaked Wood.

Brian Hamill

THE OTHER SIDE OF THE DOOR

Looking at the banister that leads me up – is it the same one I grabbed on to with the hands of a boy. I take hold of it, but that doesny bring anything back. These are definitely the same stone steps. You could get nostalgic about it, the wee feet up and down them, but generations of folk will have used these their whole lives. I haven't been here for so long of my time. They are just stairs I was on for some years, no more meaning than other flights in other places. And at the top is the front door. I will chap it and wait, if they are still living there. The mam and the dad. If they're alive. If one of them is. Which one. I go up, a few of the stairs not all, and see there's a potplant next to the door. It is small, leaves hanging out over the rim. Very green against the old wall, its paint cracked and peeling. A different colour now.

They will recognise me, and I will recognise them. Though it might take a second or two, for them. They don't expect me. Once they get past the wrinkles round the eyes and the no hair, they will tell it's their son. Faces all stay the same, even with age, nobody ends up looking like a different person. This is what I think, but really Christ knows. Maybe the eighty-year-old mammy has shrunk, and dyed her hair, and worked into her late sixties, early seventies, and had sadness, and been sick, and maybe people do come to look different after all, their faces, because what would I know, I know nothing, only impressions, guesses, what I've learned but I've not learned much, not compared to others.

No nameplate on the door. There had been one, the name my old granda handed down, and his before him, and all that. This might mean they've moved – moved or else died. Probably it's a different door, a newer one, and they decided not to nail the old plate back up. Or my da had got sick of it, pulled it off and painted over the marks. That fucking thing, giving the game away to everybody. He could've stopped wanting every Tom, Dick or Harry bastard to know whose door they were chapping. That's as I remember him, the old boy, he talked that way. If he hadn't changed too much, it's exactly the sort of stuff I see him saying, thinking, doing.

So no nameplate and a net curtain behind the glass square, frosted glass, to hide what lies within eh. Doorbell on the side. No knocker. Maybe I'd flap the letterbox. But then I wouldny hear what kind of doorbell it was, if it was a ringer or a singer. Do both. One then another. Maybe a rap on the frosted glass for good measure. Decisions. Fuck sake.

But would that mammy ever have bought a potplant and sat it at her front door. She had a thing about cats. It was a thing called hatred. Easy to imagine her if she came out and a cat had pissed on the bloody new plant. She would've considered that when she sat the pot down, the thought would surely have crossed. Unless she didny mind cats these days. Maybe she had mellowed. And I am on the landing, the stairs are done with, if I was for flapping the letterbox straight away this instant I am within prime flapping distance. But taking a minute to chew over if the wee mam might've gone a bit soft in her old age, and toward cats in particular. If the possibly dead and so now-fictional mother who possibly doesny live in that house any more might or might not have mellowed, if mellowed is the word, toward cats as a species, the cats of this neighbourhood of which there may be none whatsoever, aye exactly these such invisible, fictitious, annoying fucking cats, as only a mellowing of this sort could explain the potted plant if indeed its presence was something to do with the female person who may or may not live there, may or may not be standing on the hall carpet in her slippers this very second, aware of somebody outside, close by, with her heart beating away same as ever, blood still going round the old veins, sipping her tea calmly, keeping her nerve since she had no intention of unlocking or opening anyway, or else just a set of bones somewhere, inside a box, and there was to be nobody in this flat, if she, when she did live and was making the decision regarding the potplant, was fictional imaginary cat-piss taken into account at all, this is what should be established, if indeed it was her, whether it was a factor, whether

Christ.
Just,
the need to think, for some time to think, but looking again at the frosted glass, watch if any of the wee globules flicker and show movement behind, somewhere in the old lobby. Nothing but the net, the still net

hanging on the other side. There is a memory of me, the boy, throwing a cricket ball through the glass panel because I was lying on the steps and had hurt my foot or knee, or ankle or arse, and the mammy couldn't hear me shouting, trying to shout on her but crying. They told the story at all the family get-togethers, mam loved the telling of the moment where she saw the ball on the carpet, knew it was mine, rushed out to give me what for, then saw the wee dirty teary face, blood on the trousers, and carried me into the bath, told the da it was boys from up the flats that done it.

I don't know if I remember this happening, and me doing it and me seeing her and the glass everywhere, the kisses and the bath, the secret, or if my pictures of it were all made later, when I was older, when the mammy told it and everybody was looking and smiling, and asking me. I never know if it is real, a real memory, or made out of her story, her telling of it. What if she had exaggerated. Misremembered. Made it up. A fabrication. A load of old bollocks. A steaming pile of dogshit. Nobody can know. It could've been boys from up the flats, for all anybody cares. What boys. If she is dead, the memory doesny exist. What flats.

The net curtain is moving. Moved, slightly. Out a little, back against the frame. Soft, slight motion. A draught inside. A window somewhere is cracked open. Or was it a hand, after seeing this figure through the window and wanting to get a better look, a wee twitch of the drape with one finger, just to see if there was definitely somebody standing there or not. And what would happen if I was to flap that letterbox. If I smashed something through, for real this time, on purpose, with purpose, no boys from somewhere else, no lies needed. A concrete action. I would shatter it, give them a fright. Maybe they need a fright, being so long in there, the two of them on their own. What would happen if I put my fist clean through it, clean, into the face of whoever flicked at the curtain and is standing there now, casting a shadow over but not knowing, waiting for movement but not moving, breathing and looking but not speaking, no, not saying a thing. Breathing.

Or, if I just move forward.
If I take two more steps.

William Hershaw

THE TEMPEST: ARIEL'S SANG

Your faither ligs five faddoms ablaw,
His banes wrocht tae coral in the undertaw,
His een are aa blin and pairlie.
Nou there's naethin left o him attour,
He's undertaen a birl, a chynge,
Nou he's an unco ferlie.
Lend a lug!
The selkies ding his daith bell ilka hour.
Dinnle! Dunnle!

Lucy Ingrams

JALOPY FREEZE

Midnight and the street so bound with cold
my short walk to the car's an ice-pick. Inside,
crystalled windows igloo me and when
I turn the key it's no surprise to hear:

> *rack rack rack.*

It's fine – I have a glamourie of spells
and images to coax the battery round
for morning. Besides, the heating
works (hard to credit so much luck) and so . . .

in time . . . I see two cyclists bent
as Shackleton to a sledge, my neighbour
douse his van locks free with anti-seize, a taxi
decked with lights that passes like a party.

> *Rack rack rack –*

it's fine, I'm dressed to wait (touch
the warmth of my Nepali hat) and, from
the radio, Saharan electronica silvers
through the dark, like rising mercury. Besides,

you rang tonight: your smiling sound,
the way you teased me for leaving
raisins on my plate, recalled that frame
of sky, drew up a summer trip—

Rack rack rack.

I picture spinning circuitry, seat-sway
to the backing synth of Atlas-mountain birdsong.
I'm fine (for once), could wait out here all night,
at anchor in the ice – going nowhere, dancing.

SLOW AIR

on a theme by Robert Burns

my
   heart   my
     heart's   my

in the moor-
   land   the mainland   the low-
     lands   the islands   the high—

my heart   my
   heart's not   my heart
     isn't

is chasing   is chaste for   is
   wandering   is wan
     for   wonders after

its dear,   and where-
   ever I   ever I
     go   go now,

my dear,   not to havens   to
   lochans   not to
     forests   to firths

my
   heart   my
     heart's   my

is near you   's never
   far from   isn't
     here

Alexander Lang

INSIGNE

See yon butterflee
bleezin thair in bleck an reid
    affrontin me
wi skyrie metaphors o God

Its spredin wungs
wha's colors fret the simmer nuin
    saw aeons pass
throu chaos an a gowd cocoon

Its dusty kiss
is laid like lithograph oan stane
    wi aye saft tuch
it starts a tremor throu ma bane

Thae pupils pin
its flagrant dancin oan the wund
    it maks a pun
an leaves a hieroglyph ahin

Marcas Mac an Tuairneir

OSTAIG

Through the window of the new building,
I surveyed an ocean of opportunity;
Sparkling,
Evasive,
Like aquamarine crystal,
Liquid and molten.

Ripples,
Outfacing.

Mirage,
Blinding.

I turned from the window.
I couldn't cope with the apparition,
Enticing,
Tantalising,
Like a snowdrop dissolving;
Skittishness away with the breeze.

Marcas Mac an Tuairneir

OSTAIG

Tro uinneag an togalaich ùir,
Dh'fheuch mi cuan an dùil;
Boillsgeach,
Neo-ruigheach,
Mar dhrillsich chlach-mara,
Leaghta, leannach.

Frith-thonn
A bha tuilleadh 's a chòir.

Crith-theas
A dhall mo lèirsinn.

Thionndaidh mi bhon uinneig.
Cha do ghabh mi ri aisling
Thàlach,
Sheilleanach,
Mar bhleideag a' ruith air an uisge;
Giarag air falbh leis an osaig.

SOMETIMES

Sometimes,
It's swift,
And conquers you
With a lightning flash.

Or it can be soft,
Blossoming
Petal by petal,
Like the bud of a snowdrop.

Sometimes,
It's the breeze,
Compelling it
To lift its wilted head,

Until it looks
Into the clouds,
Shedding gentle snowfall.
It's the flake that melts
In the thimble of its flower.

Sometimes,
It's a sunflower,
Following the
Summer swelter.

With its face,
Big, black and honest,
Returning to you,
Its genesis and safety.

UAIREANNAN

Uaireannan,
The e sgiobalta;
A' bualadh ort
Mar bhalt na fàire.

No socarach;
A' blàthachadh,
Duilleag air dhuilleag,
Mar ghucag na gealaige-làir.

Uaireannan,
'S e a' ghaoth
Ga misneachadh
A ceann crom a thogail,

Gus an coimhead e
Dha na sgòthan,
A chuireas sneachda mìn.
'S a' bhleideag a leaghas
Am meuran beag a' bhlàthain.

Uaireannan,
'S e neòinean-grèine,
A' leanmhainn
Teas an t-samhraidh.

Le aodann,
Mòr-dhubh onarach,
A' tilleadh dhut,
Suaimhneas a thùis.

Sometimes,
It's exotic;
A fruit from far away,
Imperfect fit in the bowl.

Or blessed
With its sacred,
Seductive scent.
Lavender, all-pervasive,
Adding perfume to your world.

Sometimes,
It's the song-thrush,
Whose twittering
Disturbs your sleep.

And it was erstwhile,
The fox,
With its one-night charm.
Before it forsook you,
Sinuous in the undergrowth.

Sometimes,
It's the stranger
You run into
On the road.

Or the neighbour;
An omnipresent face,
That was there
All the while.

Uaireannan
Tha e allmhara,
Is na chnuasach cian-thìreil,
Nach co-fhreagair am bobhl'.

No seunta,
Leis a' chùbhrachd
Dhaorachail, naomh.
Lus na tùise, uile-sgaoilte,
A' cur boltrachas ri do shaoghal.

Uaireannan,
'S e an smeòrach,
Le a truitreach
Gad dhùsgadh bhod shuain.

Bha e aon uair
Na shionnach,
Aoileanta air an oidhche a-mhàin
Mus do chùlachadh sa mhadainn
Is e lùbach fon fho-fhàs.

Uaireannan,
'S e an strainnsear
Ris an tachair thu
Air an rathad.

No an nàbaidh;
Aodann uile-làithearach,
A bha rid thaobh,
Fad an t-siubhail.

Sometimes,
It's the only word
That can satisfy your need.
Unheard for many a year.

A faithful friend,
Returned from a far-off land,
Courting you with tales,
That'll make your world
Up-end.

Sometimes,
It's a murmur,
And your lips
Like the jittering moth.

A song,
That surpasses vocabulary,
To explain your heart's desire.
A tune that seeks a harmony
To complete its musicality.

And so,
It's a thing that cannot be performed,
By the soloist alone,
Or a choir in full song.

Though it isn't
Mathematics,
It's a question
With one right answer.

Uaireannan,
'S e am facal a-mhàin
A shàsaicheadh do dhìth.
Gun chluinntinn fad iomadh bliadhn'.

Caraid ceanalta,
Ùr-thìllte à dhùthaich chèin,
Suiridheach le sgeòil
A chuireadh do shaoghal
Caoin air ascaoin.

Uaireannan,
Tha e na na mhànran,
Is do bhilean
Mar leòmann air chrith.

Òran
Nach gabh ri briathran
Gus ciall a chur air do mhiann.
Fonn a' sireadh siansaidh
Gus co-sheirm a choileanadh.

'S mar sin,
'S e nì nach tèid a thaisbeanadh
Leis an aon-neach,
No a' chòisir shlàn.

Ged nach e
Matamataig,
'S e ceist
Gun ach aon fhreagairt cheart.

And it'll make a teenager of you,
With a bunsen to burn,
As you hold your taper to the gas,
In the school chemistry class.

It's a thing without rules;
A feeling
Without form.

It's the mistake,
You can't correct,

It's what puts your past
And future tense,
In context.

'S e a nì deugaire dhìot
Le lòchran ri lasadh,
Is tu a' cur coinnlein ri gas,
An clas ceimig na sgoile.

'S e a tha gun riaghailt;
Faireachdainn gun rian.

'S e a' mhearachd
Nach gabh a ceartachadh,

'S e a chuireas an seachad
Is an tràth teachdail
An gnìomh.

James McGonigal

LEFT–RIGHT COALITION SET TO FALL

My feet were guessing today's choice of hosiery –
black as usual, but of shades and logos variously faded.

When he was working he'd wear Marks & Spencer socks
with colour-coded heels and toes, or days of the week
          printed on
each instep. His 'diary of footsteps', ha. He even bought
          multiples
of each set in case the washer broke down, well prepared
          to march
onwards for a fortnight without fail.

Retirement days merge into one another. Now he wears
          two Tuesdays
on a Saturday and on a Wednesday it might well be Fridays.
          Not yet
the rebel chaos of un-pairing, when Monday's sock will
          syncopate
with Thursday's or Sunday dance a jig with whoever comes
          to hand.
Then we won't know if he's coming or going

or whether or when he will ever arrive.

Jen McGregor

LOST LOVE

Characters:

JOANNA (a young woman)
SATNAV (a satellite navigation system)

(JOANNA gets into her car and gets ready to drive. She is on the phone.)

JOANNA   That's great, Mum, but I can't talk now. I'm running really late.

SATNAV   **Welcome to the Invidia 900 Series Navigation System.**

JOANNA   I know, I'm really sorry but it's just that we promised we'd go to Finn's parents ages ago.

SATNAV   **To set up voice activation, please say your custom wake-up command now.**

JOANNA   I'm not a child any more!

SATNAV   **Your custom wake-up command has been saved.**

JOANNA   Oh, sh . . . sugar. No, sorry, I'm just trying to figure out this Sat Nav thing and I think I may have programmed something by accident.

SATNAV   **Please enter your destination.**

JOANNA   No, I just got it last night – early prezzie from Finn.

SATNAV   **Sorry, that destination has not been recognised. Did you mean Findhorn?**

JOANNA   No! You're being unfair.

SATNAV   **Please enter your destination.**

JOANNA   He is not being flashy, it was a very thoughtful and—

SATNAV   **Did you mean Fulton Road, Dundee?**

JOANNA   Yes it is! You might not think it's romantic but I—

SATNAV   **Thank you. Preparing your route.**

JOANNA   Ah! No no no don't do that, I'm not going there! Look, Mum, there's no point in us having this conversation just now, all right? I'm really late as it is and I have to figure out this bloody Sat Nav and—

SATNAV   **Please drive to highlighted route.**

JOANNA   Jesus Christ, Mother! Right, I'm sorry, I'm sorry, it just
          slipped out, I'm really sorry. Please, I really need to go now.

SATNAV   **Please drive to highlighted route.**

JOANNA   I know. Love you too. Have a good Christmas. See you
          tomorrow.

SATNAV   **Please drive to highlighted route.**

JOANNA   Right, now you need to get me on the right road right
          now, because I am so fucking late . . . Back . . . back . . .
          Register your device? I don't want to register, I just want
          to use the damn thing . . . Cancel. Menu . . . Personalise?
          Who personalises these fucking things? Navigate. That
          should be it.

SATNAV   **Please enter your destination.**

JOANNA   Tomcroy Terrace, Pitlochry.

SATNAV   **You entered Tomcroy Terrace, Pitlochry, PH16 5JA.
          Say yes to confirm.**

JOANNA   Yes.

SATNAV   **Thank you. Preparing your route.**

JOANNA   Come on, I am so late . . .

SATNAV   **Please drive to highlighted route.**

JOANNA   Thank you!

(*JOANNA drives.*)

SATNAV   And that was it. Our first conversation. Not what you
          might call an auspicious start, but that's how I knew. I
          mean, if you can see someone late, flustered and
          swearing at their mother and still feel this way about
          them, it must really be love! **Turn left on Tay Street.** I'd
          heard about this happening, of course. Fresh out of the
          box, falling madly for the first person to pick you up and
          switch you on. **Turn left on Atholl Street.** But it's
          different for me. I'm not a first-timer, I'm an ex-display
          model. I've been unpacked and handled and had every
          button pressed by more hands than I care to remember.
          Turn right on Dunkeld Road. And yes, there's that first
          fleeting rush when someone picks you up and you

wonder if this is going to be the one, and maybe if you're only ever operated by one person you can fool yourself into thinking you've got some kind of bond – **Turn right on A912** – because then you'll never know that crushing disappointment when they just put you back on the shelf and pick up the slightly higher-spec TomTom on the next shelf. **Continue on A912.** Maybe then it's perfectly harmonious until the day they stop updating your maps and finally just stop switching you on at all. It's fine. You'll never need to see that they've moved on to a newer model, you can gather dust in peace and – **At roundabout take second exit** – quiet.

JOANNA Second exit? Well, you're the one with the satellites . . .

SATNAV **Turn right onto Ruthvenfield Road.** So that's how I knew she was the one. And all of a sudden I knew, I just *knew* that she wouldn't mind about my past. My battered box, my slightly worn carry case, last year's maps – **Turn left onto Ruthvenfield Avenue** – none of it would matter to her! **Turn left onto Inveralmond Road.** She would *appreciate* me. **Turn right onto Ruthvenfield Road.**

JOANNA Okay . . . I have no idea what the point of that little detour was.

SATNAV **At roundabout, take first exit onto A9.**

JOANNA Nope, no point at all. Great. Exactly what I need, a bit more time spent wandering around random streets so I can be even later and Finn's parents can hate me and Finn will get more and more pissed off. So we're looking at either a Christmas break-up or a near miss. Lovely. Come on, you tosser, either speed up or get out of the bloody fast lane! And then it'll be back to Mum's to hear all about how crap a boyfriend Finn is and how crap I am for staying with him. Oh, great, and now it's snowing. Dark at four p.m. and bloody snowing. Oh, how fucking jolly.

(*She drives. She plays with the radio. The SATNAV quietly adores her. She curses other drivers under her breath.*)

SATNAV   **In five hundred yards, turn left on A822.** Not the most
          direct route – not the right route at all, in fact, but I just
          want to keep her with me.

JOANNA   What? Why are we turning off here? Right, I've had
          enough of this.

          (*She stops the car and makes a phone call.*)

          It's Joanna. Yes, I know I'm late, I'm really sorry, it's just that
          I've got a bit lost. Well, yes, but that's actually the problem
          – I'm using it right now, but I must have programmed it
          wrong or something. Oh Finn, don't be angry with me,
          please, I tried to set off on time, I really did, it's just that
          Mum phoned and you know how she— Finn, please,
          look, I'm getting on my way again now. Can you just tell
          me if you've heard about any diversions on the A9? The
          Sat Nav's just taken me down this tiny back road
          somewhere near Dunkeld and I thought— No, I haven't
          seen any signs. Okay. Thanks anyway. Be there soon. I
          love— (*He has hung up.*) Oh. Right. (*She restarts the car.*)

SATNAV   **Please drive to highlighted route. Continue on A822.**

JOANNA   If you say so . . . Christ, can't they divert us down gritted
          roads?

SATNAV   So that's Finn. Her destination . . . He's no good for her. I
          could only hear his muffled voice from her phone, but I
          can tell. How could he speak to her like that? How could
          anyone speak to *her* like that?

JOANNA   Next year we're spending Christmas in Mombasa. Sun,
          sea, no driving and no bloody families.

SATNAV   **Turn right on Unnamed Road.**

JOANNA   You cannot be serious.

SATNAV   **Turn left on Unnamed Road.**

JOANNA   There's no way this is right.

SATNAV   **Turn right on Unnamed Road.**

JOANNA   Come on, take me back to somewhere with streetlamps.

SATNAV   **Turn right on Unnamed Road.**

JOANNA   Streetlamps and signs. And no trees.

SATNAV **Turn left on Unnamed Road. You have arrived at your destination.**

JOANNA What? No I haven't!

SATNAV Oh, but you have.

JOANNA Where the hell is this?

SATNAV Better if you don't know. In fact, it would be better if I were to turn my display brightness right down.

JOANNA Shit! What's happening now?

SATNAV Down so far that you can't see the map any more.

JOANNA Oh no no no no no! Please don't do this! Restart! New destination!

SATNAV I'm afraid your command has not been recognised.

JOANNA Reboot! Restart! Help! Menu!

SATNAV **I'm afraid your command has not been recognised.**

JOANNA Shit! (*She takes out her phone.*) No signal, *shit* . . . Maybe I can find my way back to the main road.

SATNAV No, my love, it's far too dark. Not to mention icy.

JOANNA Getting turned is going to be a bloody nightmare.

SATNAV Why would you want to turn back, Joanna? What can he offer you? I love you, Joanna. Follow where I lead.

(*The car skids slightly, then recovers.*)

JOANNA Shit shit shit!

SATNAV This is the wrong way, why would you take such a treacherous path a second time?

JOANNA Really slow, that's it. Slow and careful. Breathe.

SATNAV You can't go back, Joanna.

JOANNA It'll all be okay. Just take it nice and slow . . .

SATNAV You can't.

JOANNA Calm and caref—

SATNAV **Display brightness: Maximum.**

(*JOANNA is startled. She loses control of the car. She screams.*)

This is how it has to be, my love. **You have arrived at—**

(*CRASH*)

Christopher Whyte

VUILLARD'S MOTHER

As if reality were an
old-fashioned film, his eye would pick
out squares of celluloid as one
by one they rushed powerfully

past his sight. He'd take in hand
a fine brush followed by a broad
brush, a softer or harder brush,
to remake them, carefully,

painstakingly, assisted by
the many colours he squeezed out
from the twisted, battered tubes.
The abundant patterns he saw

revealed to him in the carpets,
the wallpaper and the curtains,
besieged his mind; and here and there
he would leave the canvas or

the cardboard without any
covering, so the bareness
that remained would bear faithful
witness to the intensity

and liveliness of the impulse
that had inspired him. That was how
she made her way into his
paintings, the artist's mother,

whom he caught as he found her,
with no regard for good manners

Crìsdean MacIlleBhàin

MÀTHAIR VUILLARD

Mar gur e film air an seann dòigh
a bh' anns an fhìrinneachd, ghlacadh
a shùilean tè seach tè am measg
nan ceart-cheàrnag de *celluloid*

rachadh gu drùidhteach 'nan deann-ruith
seachad air amharc. Ghabadh e
'na làimh bruis bheag, bruis mhòr 'na dèidh,
bruis na bu bhuige no chruaidhe,

gus an ath-chruthachadh gu mall
is dìcheallach, le cuideachadh
nan iomadh dhath a dh'fhaoisgnich e
mach bho na pìoban toinnte, brùtht'.

Bha eanchainn-san fo sèiste leis
a' phailteas phàtranan foillsicht'
sna tapaisean, sa phàipear-bhall',
sna cùirteanan, is dh'fhàgadh e

an siud 's an seo a' chanabhais
no a' chairt-bhòrd gun chòmhdachadh
sam bith, air dòigh 's gum biodh an luim'
a dh'fhanadh a' toirt teisteanais

dìls' air dèine 's beothalachd
a' ghrad-smuain rinn a bhrosnachadh.
Fhuair is' a-steach do dhealbhan-san
mar sin, màthair an ealantair –

ga glacadh cuideachd mar a thuit,
gun smaoineachadh am b' iomchaidh e

or what was appropriate,
in her day's most private moments.

Her son's cold eye did not respect
the privacy or fragility
of the old woman's tranquil,
predictable, accepting life.

He used her as material,
and she allowed herself to be
used in that way. If he asked
her she would spend a full hour

holding an awkward position
that he had noticed, bent over
the stove, or adjusting the lamp,
until her son was satisfied,

until he had fixed her image
on whatever scattered sheet
of paper his hand fell upon.
But if he really wanted

to make a painting of her,
he demanded even greater
patience, more exacting effort.
He would paint her as she paused

before the mirror to arrange
the rich tresses of her hair,
balancing her ledger-book,
or as she sewed by the window

no modhail, anns na mòmaidean
na bu phriobhaidiche dhe là.

Cha robh sùil fhuar a mic a' caomhnadh
dìomhaireachd no anfhannachd
na beatha foisnich, cunbhalaich,
muinghinich a bh' aig a' chaillich.

Dh'ùisnich e mar stuth i, agus
dheònaich ise a bhith cleachdte
mar sin. Nan rachadh iarraidh oirr',
stadadh i fad uarach ann

an suidheachadh neo-sgiobalta
a bha e air mothachadh dhà,
crom air an stòbh', no ceartachadh
na làmpa, gus am biodh a mac

riaraichte, gus na shocraich e
a h-ìomhaigh-se air duilleig sgapt'
air choreigin, thachair fo làimh.
Ach nam b' e a dealbhadh-se

gu ceart a bha 'na rùn, b' fhaide
's bu dhuiliche na b' fheudar dhi
chur ris dhe shaothair 's fhoighidinn.
Bhitheadh e ga peantadh, 's i

'na suidhe ron sgàthan, a falt
saidhbhir, fada ga rèiteachadh,
no deasachadh a cunntasan, no
fuaigheil ri taobh na h-uinneige,

where she could get all the light
that she needed for her work,
or, at breakfast time with her grandchild
positioned in a highchair

beside her, while the grandmother
gave her a piece of food, their two
round heads coming close together,
as if they had been balls that were

of different dimensions.
Gradually he prepared an
exhaustive tribute to her life
with care, constancy, full awareness.

He never had to look beyond
the rooms where they lived together,
but found everything that
he wanted in the humble,

unassuming lives that touched
upon his own existence.
Every hidden mystery,
each majesty and horror

was expressed in the silent
interwoven patterns of
the curtains, or the tenacious
conduct of his mother, in

the repeated rituals of
the silent sacrament she kept

far am faigheadh i an leus
a bha feum aice air, air neo
aig àm na bràcaiste, a h-ogh'
stèidhichte an seathar àrd

aig a taobh, 's an t-seanmhair chaomh
a' toirt dhi pìos beag bidh', an dà
chinn chruinn a' dlùthachadh ri chèil'
mar gur e bàllaichean a bh' ann,

ach toimhsean eadar-dhealaicht' ac'.
Dh'ullaicheadh leis uidh air n-uidh
moladh coileanta dhe beatha
le faicill, diongmhaltas is rùn.

Cha robh feum air a bhith sealltainn
taobh thall nan rumannan san robh
iad beò le chèile. Gheibheadh e
gach eileamaid a bha feumail

sna beathannan a bheanadh ri
a bheatha fhèin, 's iad iriseal,
neo-uallach. Bha gach rùn-dìomhair,
gach mòrachd agus uabhasachd

gan cur an cèill am pàtranan
nan cùirtean, eadar-fhight', tostach,
no an dèanadas leanailteach
a mhàthar, ann an gnàthachadh

ath-nuadhaichte na sacramaid
bailbh a chum i là seach là,

each day with no trace of show
or fuss. His tribute was offered

to someone who was as foreign,
strange and different as could be,
someone who did not feel the spur
that gave him no rest, goading

him to surpass reality,
making it cleaner, more perfect,
reworking, rediscovering.
He couldn't stop himself from

forever adding to it,
while his mother herself was
satisfied with reality
that filled her out completely.

Translated by Niall O'Gallagher

gun lorg air spailp no ùpraid. Bha
am moladh sin ga thairgse leis

gu neach a bha cho coigreach, galld'
is diofaraicht' 's a ghabhadh, neach
nach robh a' faireachdainn a' bhruid
nach leigeadh e ri fois, a rinn

a spreigeadh gus an fhìrinneachd
a dhèanamh na bu soillsich', na
bu ghlaine, gu h-ath-shaothrachadh,
h-ath-cheannsachadh. Cha b' urrainn dhà

gun a bhith a' sìor chur rithe
ged a bha a mhàthair mhàlda
sàsaichte leis an fhìrinneachd,
ga lìonadh gu h-iomlan leatha.

Lorn Macintyre

BARROWLAND

For Jimmy McMahon

The day I bought a Dansette blew my mind.
It was at the Barras, from a big man blind
in one eye 'frae a razor chib', a woman beside me
said. 'He wuz in the Cow Toi, an awfy mob, ye ken.
Where de ye come frae son? The west, ye say?
Gae canny; there are still hooligans in this city.'
(This was 1960, when I arrived for university,
before tenements were flattened for a motorway.)
I got the Dansette for three quid, and that same day
I went to Rex for my first Rock & Roll EP,
yep, you've guessed – Bill Haley and His Comets.
I was in Maclay Hall in Park Terrace,
rooming with a musical medic from the Congo,
and when I played 'Rock Around the Clock'
on the Dansette he supplied backing on his bongos.
When the bedroom of the residence began to shake
he yelled: 'Let's hit Glasgow with an earthquake!'

I practised swivelling my hips to the Comets' beat,
then took the tram to a tailor in Renfield Street,
enquiring about made-to-measure Teddy Boy gear.
The man knelt beside me, as if fitting out a knight
for the Crusades. 'Sir, you require a velvet collar,
the same on the cuffs, the trousers not too tight
because you don't want to constrict your testicles.'
The flanneller threw in a bootlace tie for nothing.
I bought blue suede shoes in the Emporium,
then went to have my hair styled in a salon
in West Nile Street where the scissors flitted,
silver birds above the heads of the clientele,
the radio playing Twitty's 'It's Only Make Believe'.

'What's it to be, son?' the barber asked. 'A trim?'
'No, a duck's arse please,' I said self-consciously.
He was smirking in the big mirror as he began
the conspicuous show of his artistry.

The Teddy Boy suit a perfect fit, crepe soles
squeaking along Bath Street, I boarded a tram,
swaying through the mild October evening
along Argyle Street to the Gallowgate, alighting
at the neon sign proclaiming BARROWLAND.
Straight from her shift, a clippie, blonde hair
in big rollers under her headsquare,
a new frock with dance shoes in a holdall.
A bouncer stopped me in the entrance hall.
'Any trouble, Teddy, and you'll be fleein'
doon the stairs on the toe o' ma shoe.'
The floor was as big as Hampden stadium,
jumping, hundreds of dancers, the women
cool in all colours, most of the men
in suits and shirt-sleeves, Teddy Boys
in brothel creepers and luminous socks.
A good-looker grabbed me: 'Let's rock!'

Females were being hoisted by the waists,
birled under arms, crouching, sliding
across the floor as if on roller skates, gliding
between their partners' splayed feet,
hands waving, fingers snapping to the beat
of Billy MacGregor and the Gaybirds,
the trombone's golden piston lubricated
by the sweat of the dancers. I waited

to ask a redhead to teach me to rock.
She looked me up and down and said:
'Ah widnae be seen deid wi' a Ted.'
I went on the floor with a brunette instead,
and afterwards fetched her a lemonade,
sitting with her on a sofa, until her boyfriend
brought a promising conversation to an end.
Maybe I missed a chibbing: who knows?
Or a kicking from winkle-picker toes.

I spent the rest of the evening rocking,
my heart going with the pounding drum,
my legs in and out to the irresistible rhythm,
my partners airborne, knickers showing.
After the last dance, the saxophone laid
in its case, shimmering cymbal quietening.
I was sad, wanting it to go on till dawn.
Out on the mean street I boarded a tram,
but couldn't sleep for the adrenalin.
The beat had got into my blood.
Night after night I was out dancing,
Barrowland, Dennistoun Palais, the Majestic.
Was I neglecting my studies? But hey!
I was a student of philosophy, and found
the embodiment of John Stuart Mill's
'Greatest happiness for the greatest number'
in Barrowland, my spiritual home.

One evening I was blessed with a lumber,
snogging the girl in a nearby close, until
a door opened, an old woman shuffling.
Instead of putting her ashes in the bin

they were chucked where we were necking.
Cinders burned holes in her bonnie blue dress,
like the sky at dusk when the stars appear.
From the face I'd kissed I wiped the tears.
Was the old bitch gaga, or was it malice?
Rock & Roll was swept away by the Twist.
I was in the thick of it, elbows and feet
going, so many shoes keeping to the beat.
I played Chubby Checker in the Hall
until a divinity student hammered on the wall.
Oh life was wonderful, my happiness complete,
going home near midnight on a rocking tram
before the rails were levered from the streets.

I knew that I was a student of Taoism
as well as a habitué of the ballrooms,
a saffron robe instead of Teddy Boy gear.
Dancing's like that philosophy: to attain
a state of stillness and calm that will remain
the following day, until that night's dancing,
when you recharge the energy again,
the difference being that you use jiving
instead of meditation to reach *jing*.
When the neon signs of Glasgow's ballrooms
were switched off, one by one, I didn't pine.
The Locarno's revolving stage brings round
the night's second band's incredible sound;
Billy MacGregor and the Gaybirds thrill;
in the Dennistoun the beat pounds on;
and in the Flamingo, with the giant effigy
of that bird winging overhead, I'm flying still.

Alan Mackay

HOTEL TERMINAL

Ends of lines have their own melancholy, their own half-forgotten pain. Here, on the edge of the desert, ten miles from the dunes and six hundred from the nearest coast, a particular pain bleaches in the furnace light of the sun.

*

The bellhop, the one with the strangulated voice and the too-long neck that seems to underline the choking gutturals of his speech, sits in the shade, playing ping-pong with the flies against the white stucco of the hotel's wall. He speaks no English, only a smattering of French, some Spanish, borne on a caravan out of that part of Morocco some decades before, and a very little Tuareg. For the most part he speaks one of the dialects of the language of this borderless country on the edge of nowhere, and smiles.

*

When the bus pulled in here from who cares where, and the driver switched off its clatter-bucket engine then slipped off into the near-deserted market, I sat in a perfect peace. At first all I felt was the silence, the utter stillness of the desert's afternoon, then I heard the flies as I sat in the oven of the ancient Mercedes-Benz bus. This is the end of the line, the bus and I go no further. We have only going back to look forward to here, only the returns.

*

The bellhop, when he tires of his sport with the flies, plays another game. He enters the hotel and walks towards the reception desk with slow and purposeful steps until, at the last moment, just before the reception clerk's head flicks up, he swerves aside and walks to the kitchen door. I have seen him do this now countless times. The reception clerk merely drops his head to his ledgers, turning pages back and

forward, noting names on a sheet of paper and blowing sideways the
flies from his mouth.

*

The first evening I ate in the dining room of the hotel. Onion soup, a
stew of goat and vegetables and a beer. The other guests entered one
by one and sat alone, or together, there seemed to be no scheme to it,
around the room. Some of them struck up conversation across the
silence between the tables as the tall black waiters glided between them
bearing the huge tureen and ladle like a sacrament.

Over by the door to the foyer a girl, of the most singular beauty, sat
patient as the procession wove its pattern about the room. I was unable
to take my eyes from her. She sat demure, her hands folded on her lap,
her body turned slightly away from me so that I saw her half in profile.
She wore a traditional robe from the market, bright colours in bold
multi-width stripes, loose and airy against the persisting heat. Around
her head she had wound a length of pale blue muslin from which fine
threads of auburn hair escaped.

—Is it onion again? she asked.

The waiter nodded.

—Very well then, she said, and smiled.

*

Sometimes the bellhop, tired of baiting the unheeding hotel clerk, will
step outside the hotel, onto the verandah, and scratch his balls through
the loose cotton of his trousers. On these occasions he scratches with
an unconscious pleasure, smiling as he scans the street from end to
end and back again while happily clawing at his scrotum. He is, I have
discovered, a man of very simple pleasures and wants.

*

The next evening, I think it was the next evening, time so conspires
against the order of my mind in this place that I cannot be sure.
Whatever, one evening shortly after my arrival, I took my meal in
the town, down by the market. Here the food was both cheaper and

better. A soup of vegetables and a stew of chicken with rice that snapped softly between my teeth. Here they do not sell beer as this is forbidden by the religion which seems to exist outside the hotel. On my way back to the hotel I saw the girl walking by the old legion fort around which the town had grown. She wore another robe, pale blue this time, like the turban from the first time I had seen her. I counted her steps, thirty-seven of them, until she disappeared from my sight, then walked over and looked at her footprints in the sand until the evening wind erased them.

*

There was great excitement in the hotel one day soon after my arrival. The bellhop dashed around the foyer and dusted anything which did not appear to move. The hotel manager, who usually kept to his office and its lazy overhead fan, appeared after breakfast wearing a dark suit and collar and tie. His excitement could not conceal his discomfort, however, and the perspiration ran down his face and stained his collar.

—A visitor is coming, he said, to no one in particular. —A visitor to the town.

Staff I had not seen before appeared and busied themselves in clumsy ways about the foyer and the dining room. They moved furniture from one place to another and then back again. They swept dust into piles in one corner, then transferred it to another, and another until the dust had visited all corners of the room and had been replaced by more dust from the street. At one point several of the hotel guests were asked to lift their feet from the floor in order that the dust may complete its journey, myself included. I eased myself from my chair and went outside to escape the lunacy. To my left, the girl sat writing in her journal and we exchanged smiles. I turned to my right and sat in the wicker chair by the door.

There was no lunch served that day, the guests who had not gone to the dunes gathered as usual, but no lunch was served. Outside the staff were hanging bunting along the front of the hotel, ribbons and tapes in the colours of the national flag, and were too busy to serve us. We stood and watched. The girl had gone inside to her room. The day droned on and slowly the staff drifted inside to escape the heat. No more preparations could be made.

The bellhop stood outside in one of his dreams, scratching at his groin and staring out to the west into the rippling haze of the late afternoon. Out there, on the edge of the shimmer, a cloud began to form of dust. The bellhop stopped his scratching and peered out along the line of the road, shading his eyes with one hand.

—*Arrivé*, he cried, turning and beaming at me. —*Arrivé*!

He ran inside calling to the staff. A desultory group of guests began to drift out of the hotel and onto the verandah. The girl was not among them. I went inside and asked the clerk for her room number and went upstairs.

—The visitor is coming, I called through her door. —There is a cloud of dust on the horizon.

—Thank you for telling me, she called. —But I have been disappointed here before by promises of visitors. I will watch from my window. Thank you anyway. Her voice sounded so far away from me that it was almost as if she was not there at all, just a memory of another voice and another room. The limits on the permutations of events catches up on me at moments like those and leaves me with such a feeling of aching emptiness. I marvel at my capacity to persevere.

I went downstairs and joined the group on the verandah. The cloud had now reached the edge of town and the street had begun to fill with people all wearing bright and colourful clothes. The children had been ushered from their school, each one clutching a miniature of the national flag fashioned from twigs and crayoned paper. The air of expectation and stifled excitement was palpable. The hotel manager stood in front of his staff at the top of the short flight of stairs from the street to the verandah, his hands clasped before him and the nervous calm of his temporary importance clenched upon his face.

With a roar a convoy of military vehicles swept into the town; an armoured car, a personnel carrier and two jeeps; a huddle of dust-covered figures in each jeep and pennants streaming from aerials. The children waved their flags and watched as the paper blew from its flimsy contact with the twigs and into the street. The adults waved enthusiastically, I could just hear cheering over the sound of the vehicles. And then they were gone.

The manager stood proudly at the top of the stairs as the cloud of dust draped itself across his shoulders. He turned and beamed at his staff and they smiled back. The townspeople stood in small groups – large groups can be mistaken for a riot in this country – and talked animatedly at each other; the children were led back to school. We guests looked at each other in mild surprise. I realised why the girl had remained in her room. End-of-the-line places do not detain those who merely pass through.

I went to the bar for a beer and stood for a while listening to conversation wheeling around me, talk of the dunes and such, and of when the next bus may arrive or depart. The thought of it all began to depress me and so I went back outside to the now deserted street, where far to the east, a little cloud of dust lingered then faded as though it had never been. I resolved to visit the dunes one day soon.

*

One evening soon after the visit, I returned to the hotel after dinner at the market, and saw the girl sitting in the foyer reading beneath the flickering generator light. I bought a beer and sat where I could watch her without being observed. I counted the pages as she turned them, one by one. Forty-four. She closed the book and placed it on the table at her side. Then, as if to a signal, the lights went out and the silence filled the space left by the insistent noise of the generator. In the darkness the waiters scurried round lighting candles and slowly, pool by flickering pool, the room was half-filled with light. The girl sat still in her chair, her eyes tight shut and her arms stretched out along its arms. I rose and walked towards her and touched her shoulder.

—They've lit the candles.

—Have they? Thank you. Her eyes opened and they were the palest, most distant blue. —I hate when that happens, she said.

—The generator?

—And the noise the waiters make lighting the candles. Furtive. Light should not be furtive. Thank you for telling me. She pushed herself from the chair and lifted the candlestick from where the waiter had placed it on her table. —Goodnight, she said, and walked towards the stairs.

After she had gone I sat in her chair and picked up her book. It was wafer thin, hardly a book at all, *The Bridge of San Luis Rey*. I opened to the first page – *Part One: Perhaps an Accident*.

*

The other morning I found some pencil marks on the wall by my bed. They were in the form of seven-bar gates. Marking the passage of time. I just cannot recall if it was I who made them. I just cannot recall.

*

Everyone here goes to the dunes eventually. I have not felt the need. What they all seem to get out of going there, being there, I get here, in the town. Now, however – it is not that I am growing tired of the town, I have so little sense of how long I have been here that it is no longer an issue – now, I have an urge to go there, to visit them. Perhaps an urge is too strong, perhaps it is just a curiosity that I have. A curiosity that has grown inside me as to not only what the dunes are like physically, their beauty, their loneliness, their sense of loss and their pain at loss, but a curiosity as to what it is that the others find there and if that is different in any way from what I find in this terminus town. Tomorrow I will go to the dunes. I have arranged it with the hotel.

*

In the morning the bellhop wakes me with a cup of stewed tea softened with tinned milk. Outside the light is only beginning to enter the sky.

The jeep bounces and slithers on the track that leads to the dunes.

—Camel men meet us at end of the track, says the driver. —Take you to the best places. Safari.

Wrapped in my sleeping bag I can only nod my head. The cold of the desert eats into me. I am suddenly aware that in all the time I have been here, however long it may now be, I have never experienced this time of day. The faintest strands of light, out to the east, crook a finger to the sky, and the town slips into the dim behind us.

Where the camel men meet us, blue-clad Tuaregs, their faces masked
in arrogant modesty, the jeep turns and stops.

—One day? Two day? How many day? asks the driver.

—One day, I say. —Tomorrow, this time.

—Okay, he says, and helps me get my pack and sleeping bag down
from the jeep. It is hot now, the sun higher. —Bye-bye, he smiles and
lets the clutch out with a jolt and I wince.

I am motioned over to where a camel kneels beside a leafless shrub,
its jaws moving with a monotonous rhythm. My belongings are
taken from me and tied to another beast tethered to another shrub. I
mount my camel and we begin our lurching caravan out into the dunes.
The day progresses, a cavalcade of discomfort. There is nothing out
here for me.

In the afternoon we make camp at least two hours before the sun
will set. We are just below the crest of a dune, its edge a sharp silhouette
against the western sky. One of the Tuaregs walks with me to the skyline.
On the way we pass a trail of discarded cola cans and food packages,
spoor of a kind.

We sit on the very edge of the dune, its face below us dropping away
at our feet into a gathering gloom. Across the desert, the sun's bottom
arc begins to touch the line of the ground, ushering in the night.

Despite myself I am affected by the view. I glance to my side where
the Tuareg sits at ease, his legs crossed and his eyes, seemingly fixed
on the horizon, lost behind the shelter of his veil. One by one, the
infinity of stars begin to appear.

Later, I lie by the fire, wrapped in a blanket inside my sleeping bag
and staring at the sky. All I can think about is my stumble out into the
sand after dinner to leave my coil of excrement with a thousand others
in the darkness, an infinity of crap defiling the purest of places. I yearn
for the reassurance of my hotel room.

*

Yesterday, if not the yesterday before today, then another yesterday,
the bellhop was injured while crossing the road outside the hotel.
How it happened was like this. Across the road is a fruit stall run by a
woman who wears the same type of robe as the girl. The bellhop

seems to fancy her and often walks across the road to talk to her and buy a slice of melon for one of the hotel guests. On this occasion the girl had sent him across and she became impatient when he took too long talking to the woman who runs the stall.

—For Christ's sake, hurry up. She waved him impatiently towards her.

The bellhop jumped as if startled by an explosion, an exaggerated movement like in some gruesome silent movie. He turned and ran, without looking, across the street straight into the path of a pick-up truck. There was a dull sound and all the eyes of the hotel guests on the verandah followed the flight of the melon slice as it climbed towards the sky, then curving, fell to the dusty road beside the bellhop and burst in a deep red shower beside his head. The girl stood frozen on the edge of the verandah, her arm locked in the gesture of summons and her mouth open in a silent scream. Two men from the hotel ran past her and helped the bellhop to his feet. I walked towards the girl and put my arm across her shoulders.

—He's okay. Don't worry. I withdrew my arm, suddenly embarrassed by the intimacy of the gesture.

The girl had closed her mouth. Her arm had resumed a more natural position by her side. She turned and looked at me.

—Thank you. Again. I'd have stayed like that for ever, I'm sure.

The bellhop stood in the road, surrounded now by onlookers, shaking his head and rubbing his thigh. The girl, satisfied that he would not die, turned to re-enter the hotel.

—Should I get you another piece of melon? I asked.

—No, thank you, she said. —I have no appetite.

I watched her disappear into the darkness of the hotel, the last words of her book sounding in my head:

Even memory is not necessary for love. There is a land of the living and a land of the dead, and the bridge is love, the only survival, the only meaning.

Tomorrow I must try to leave.

David Shaw Mackenzie

THE SERVANT

He was almost sure it was a teddy bear. There were three little yellow arcs above the woman's hands and two below. At first glance, even when she was more than twenty yards away, he was almost certain that what she was carrying, pressed against her stomach, was a very small teddy bear.

And he was right. She walked slowly towards him, pacing evenly along the concrete slabs of the almost deserted Underground platform. He became aware of what she was wearing only later. At first it was just the teddy bear, the three yellow arcs above her white hands being the crown and ears and the two below being its feet. It was facing outwards, its back against her stomach, and he felt uneasy about it. This was not a girl; this was a grown woman in her mid-twenties and she was holding a teddy bear that he was sure did not belong to any child nor was a gift for one.

He turned and stared across the track at the advertising poster on the far wall of the tunnel. The woman walked towards him.

The advertisement was for a type of beauty product which seemed to be a cross between a hair shampoo and a dye. Wash your hair and make it blonder. He read all the text, or at least his eyes passed across the words. He took none of it in. He was aware only of the woman's approach. When she was quite near he stepped back to let her pass in front of him but she did not do this.

There were two or three people at the far end of the platform – the end the woman had come from – but none in the other direction. She was standing closer to him now than social convention would normally permit. He took another half-step backwards but as he did so, she began to speak.

She said, 'Excuse me,' and he said, 'Yes?'

But he knew as he glanced quickly at her face that this was not to be an enquiry about trains; he thought there might be a request for money.

'Can I speak to you?' she asked.

'Well . . .' he said, glancing at her again.

'It's just that I don't want you to be upset or angry or aggressive with me, that's all. Is that all right?'

'Go on,' he said, with no enthusiasm. He looked at the floor, the concrete slabs, saw her rope-soled canvas shoes, the hem of her red cotton wrap-around skirt.

'Do you know Jesus Christ?'

So it was God, as he should have guessed.

He managed to move his eyes higher; they reached the teddy bear. One of her fingers was twitching slightly, her hands not clasped but lying one upon the other, palm of right hand on back of left, palm of left upon the small, rather worn teddy bear.

'He's coming back,' she said, although he had not replied to her question.

He noticed she was wearing chocolate-brown nail varnish.

'He asked me to tell you.'

He looked at her face and she held his gaze for almost two seconds. A fringe of blonde hair, pale complexion, a few lines at the eyes suggesting she was older than the twenty-five he'd thought at first. No makeup. Lips that rarely smiled.

'Why you,' she said, 'I don't know. But he said you, so I'm telling you because I am his servant.'

A moment later she said, 'That's all.'

She turned away. Without a further word she began to walk at the same slow pace back down the platform towards the far end. He saw her hair, pale blonde and rather lank, reaching down to a small blue rucksack and spilling over the top of it. He watched her go, the hem of the red cotton skirt disturbed by her heels as she moved away. The poster informed him about blonde hair and how to make it blonder and he read it again, still failing to register the words at all.

He smiled at the blonde blonde girl, the two square metres of her smiling face, her cascades of hair, fingers of her right hand fanning it out for everyone to see, for everyone to know and want and need. He became aware of the movement of air from left to right before and behind him, the fluttering of a small corner of the poster, blonde paper hair blowing in the breeze, the air stronger and stronger, as the train approached, pushing the air before it.

And as he turned slowly, anticipating the train, seeing its lights in the tunnel, he caught sight of movement in front of it, movement across the lights, something red, then a sudden harsh mechanical shout from the train wheels and a hard thump, something solid hitting something solid and he fell to his knees on the platform as he realised that the woman with the teddy bear had just thrown herself in front of the train.

*

He told the police everything. He sat in the small, cluttered station-master's office with its heavy smell of cigarettes and he was shaking so much that someone brought him a cup of tea and asked him if he wanted to lie down.

After twenty minutes or so he felt calmer and found that he wanted to tell them again, the whole thing, from the moment he had first conjectured about the teddy bear until the flash of red cotton in the train lights. He wanted to tell them because surely there were details he had missed, details whose significance they would know the secret of.

He wanted to know where she was from, if she had friends and family. He wondered if she might have a child but thought it unlikely. What he didn't want to know was how broken her body was. She was dead and he knew there were no degrees of death but he felt that if he believed hard enough then there might be after all. Her injuries might be so great that they challenged the very vocabulary of death. He felt bereaved. The police told him he was in shock.

After a while he stopped shaking and they let him go.

*

When he left, the station was still closed. Red-and-white tape barred the public from entry. He went across the street to a café and sat by the window. He drank coffee and watched the station entrance.

It was half an hour before the station reopened. He reckoned it up. It was about an hour in all, perhaps an hour and five minutes, from the woman's suicide to the resumption of normal service. That was all. But appointments had been missed, meetings had been cancelled and dinners had gone cold or had curled and dried in the oven. Some people would have missed their favourite TV programmes. Someone would have said, 'I was late because some selfish fucking bastard jumped in front of my fucking train.'

He crossed the street and went back into the station.

At the bottom of the escalator he stood for a few moments in the hallway from which a short tunnel led to the platform. He approached warily and put a hand out against the white tiles of the tunnel wall to steady himself. He couldn't remember which end of the platform this tunnel led to and felt that some preparation was needed just in case he found himself suddenly at the very spot from which the woman had flung herself before the train. But when he finally stepped onto the platform he was at the other end, the end where he had been standing alone when the woman approached him. He looked across the track and the other woman, the one with the very blonde hair, was there as before, with her fixed smile.

A train burst into the station and he stepped back from the platform edge. Only half a dozen passengers got off. The train doors snapped shut and the train clattered from the station, trailing with it its noise and its wind and tunnel debris.

When the platform was empty again he began to walk down to the other end. He walked very slowly. The arrival of a group of five people, chatting and laughing, comforted him and enabled him to move forward confidently.

He reached the place from where the woman had jumped and looked down at the place where she had died.

There was nothing to see. He wasn't sure what he'd expected but there was nothing to see. The grease-blackened stones and the polished surface of the track lines were the same here as anywhere else. For a moment he wondered if he had come to the wrong platform. But this was the right place; this was the spot. He looked down at the track until he could feel the air from the next train breathing across his face. Then he turned away. On his right, as he walked back along the platform, there was a wooden bench and beside it, a litter bin. The bin was full of empty drink cans and old newspapers and, sitting on top of all this mess, the teddy bear.

*

He picked it up and looked at it. It was a small, old teddy bear, a bit worn but quite clean. There was a manufacturer's tag sewn into the seam on its right side but the lettering was too faded, the tag too furled with age for him to decipher any name.

He replaced the teddy bear in the bin and walked away. But after a few steps he turned back and picked it up once more, not knowing why he had done this. He had no bag, nothing to carry it in. He pushed it inside his jacket, its face pressed hard against his chest, and he buttoned his jacket up tight, up to the throat. Then he made his way to the end of the platform, to the escalators, the station exit and out into the gentle early evening air.

Victoria MacKenzie

TALKING ABOUT LOBSTERS

The lobsters walk at night, their ten stubby legs lumbering over gravel and sand, picking their way through dense kelp forests. They're determined wee tanks, blundering forward in search of prey, smelling through their feet, just like houseflies. Most people don't know or care about this night-time migration, too busy with their own lives behind curtains and double-glazing. But I'm a lobsterman and even when I'm sleeping I dream of lobsters, imagining them walking into my creels, lured by the chunks of stinking fish I've tied inside. When you're tucked up in your bed, take a moment to think of them, millions of them, at their night-walking.

My boat is the *Merry Jackie*, named for my wife who's less merry than she used to be. I've brought my son Martin along to check the creels with me today. He's fourteen and I wish I could say he's a good lad but I don't know if he is or not. It's the first day of the Easter holidays and I'm not letting him fester indoors, getting in his mother's way. I told him he was coming with me, and he didn't argue. Perhaps he wanted to get out the house: the atmosphere can be pure poison if Jackie's in one of her moods.

My da was a lobsterman and it was taken for granted I'd be one too. It's different these days, kids are free to make their own choices. There's no money to be made lobstering now anyway. Jackie's taken a cleaning job at the college so we can keep up with the mortgage. Martin's into computers and that's a growing market. Well, he's into computer games, but maybe it'll lead to a career. Parents have to hope.

It's a braw day, but Martin goes green as soon as we're out the harbour. You need a strong stomach to be a lobsterman and not just for the sea: the bait's rancid as hell but it gets the lobsters' attention. I tell Martin to get chopping and to look out for dolphins; maybe it'll cheer him up to see a couple of bottlenoses following us. Dolphins and porpoises are a regular part of my view and I even see pods of minke whales in summer. Some days I think there's no better life, and some days I think there's no worse. Hauling the creels is back-breaking, even with the winch doing most of the work. Each creel has a lump of concrete to weigh it down and keep it steady on the rocks, so they're not the easiest things to manoeuvre. You have to get in synch with the waves, the rise and fall.

Martin hates hauling so I get him to do the 'picking': lifting lobsters out of the creels and putting rubber bands round the claws. Lobsters are built to fight, with one claw for cutting, the other for crushing. If we don't band them, by the time we get ashore we'll only have the biggest, strongest lobster left alive and even he'll be missing a few legs.

All my creels are marked with buoys – plastic bottles mostly, nothing fancy. The first one we haul up has Martin calling out, 'Hey Da, look at this one!'

'What is it, son?' He holds a battered wee bruiser to show me and there's a leg where one of its eyes should be. 'Keep 'im,' I say. 'We'll gie him to Billy, he's no' fussed.' Billy runs the Lobster Shack, a wee café near the harbour.

'Aw Da, it's gross! He looks like an alien.' Martin lifts his own leg close to his face and waggles it about. I can't help laughing.

'Billy can make a soup or summat, no one'll ken. He'll taste as good as the rest.'

There aren't many boats on the water today. I'm one of the last lobstermen, we're a dying breed and that's not a good feeling. The waters round here used to be thick with herring but any silver light you see now is only the sun on the water. All that's left to fish is lobster and crab, and they're both getting scarce. No one knows why. It's easy to blame over-fishing, but I don't reckon that's the answer. We're careful: we throw back the females with eggs, as well as any lobsters that are too big or small. Too big and you might be taking out a major breeder, too small and they haven't had their chance yet. We've all got to have our chance.

'Da, can we have a break now?' I can tell by the whine in Martin's voice that he's flagging. We've checked twenty creels so far, and there's another eighty to go. We've only had two keepers including the freaky one with a leg where its eye should be.

'All right, son. We'll have a wee sit-doon.' I cut the engine and reach for my bag. I hold up a ham piece but Martin pulls a face.

'Got anything else?'

'Snickers suit you, sir?'

'Yep.'

I chuck it over and he eats it in three bites. He's half a foot taller than his mother already.

The two keepers are edging round their container, their whiskery antennae trying to work out where they are. I don't feel sorry for them, not really. Their brains are no bigger than a grain of rice so they can't feel pain, not like us.

Martin's looking at his phone but there's no signal out here.

'Expecting a call, son?' I ask.

He ignores me. He was a right chatterbox as a lad, full of jokes and always reciting bits of comedy shows. Now he never says a word. People say give them time and they'll come back to you, but I miss him. And I can't help worrying. Lobsters are more upfront about things: they communicate by squirting urine in each other's faces. None too sweet, but I've seen worse outside The Ship on a Saturday night.

Lobsters can only grow larger by shedding their shells. Without them they're floppy as newborn kittens. They eat their old shell and bury what they can't manage, and then hide until a new one builds up round them. I wonder if they're pleased to escape their shells, those tightly soldered boxes. Perhaps they stretch out their pale bodies, exposing every soft cranny to the cold salt water, and feel a sense of relief. Maybe it's like working in an office and having your two-week holiday once a year.

We get back to work, me hauling, Martin picking and banding. We get plenty of things besides lobsters in the creels: brown crabs, which I can sell, rock cod and pollock which we use as bait. I'm getting more octopuses these days too, but I tip the creels up and let them slide back into the water. There's something about an octopus that makes me feel sad.

The wind's picking up and Martin's looking green again. 'Ready to go home, son?' I ask. He nods grimly. I turn the boat around and head back towards the harbour. It's still early in the season; the creels can wait another day. As we speed up and start bouncing across the waves, Martin asks, 'Da, are you and Mum getting divorced?'

His question blindsides me. 'Where the hell's that come from?' I
look at him, trying to fathom the way his mind's working. It's probably
all the telly he watches, soaps are full of divorces. 'Has your mum said
summat?' I ask, my voice suddenly hoarse.

'Nut.'

'Why you asking, then? Me and your mum are fine.'

He stares out to sea, his eyes narrowed against the wind. He reminds
me of my da, of pictures of him when he was just a lad himself: high
cheekbones and a shock of blonde hair that'll never lie flat.

Things aren't great between me and Jackie, I'll give Martin that, but
what marriage is when you're twenty years down the line and both
chock-full of worries?

'I love your mum, and she loves me, you've nowt to fret over.'

'She says it's your fault we're broke. You lost Grandda's boat.'

What he says is true, I did lose my da's boat, and I'll never forgive
myself. It was four years ago, just after he died. I took his death badly,
stopped doing anything much. Worse than that, I got lazy about the
boat. Before the season started I used to spend a lot of time on her:
caulking, sanding, painting. But that spring I just sat in the pub or
went down to the kirkyard and stared at his grave. I couldn't believe
he'd gone, he was only sixty-eight. Who'd I lobster with now? It's a
two-man job at heart. Martin was only ten and I didn't want him to be
a lobsterman. You want more for your kids than you've had yourself.

There's a lot of fishermen buried in that kirkyard. In storms the
seawater washes over the stone dykes and right into the graves. I was
sitting there watching the rain moving in from the east and feeling like
I wanted to disappear. Then I took it into my head to take the boat
out. Not to go lobstering, the season hadn't started, just to get out on
the water. I'd spent thousands of hours with my da on his boat – maybe
I thought I'd feel close to him again. But I knew as soon as I left the
harbour the boat wasn't right. The water was up to my ankles before I
even realised she was taking in. Fear sluiced through me and I jumped
over the side. I'd had a few drams that day but made it to the beach
somehow. When I looked up the boat was gone.

We had to remortgage the house to pay for a new one. It was insured,
of course, but Jackie insisted I get a fibreglass boat, one that wouldn't

develop any wee holes and sink. Trouble was, the next few years we
had cold springs and there were far fewer lobsters around.

'Aye son.' It's all I can say to Martin. The boy knows the truth, no
point trying to hide it. 'I did lose your grandda's boat, but that's in
the past.'

'It's not though, cos we're still broke.'

I can't answer him. I think about what it would be like, to separate
from Jackie, and I shiver.

As we approach the harbour I see something strange up on the beach.
Getting closer, I see it's a seagull and a lobster fighting. The lobster
must have escaped from someone's catch. It seems to have the upper
hand, waving his huge navy claws, keeping the bird at a distance.

'Look at that, son!' It's like something from a Roman gladiator show
scaled down. But then suddenly the gull nips in with his big yellow
beak and flips the lobster onto his back.

'Uh-oh,' Martin whispers.

The gull jabs the lobster's belly and those powerful claws stop moving.

'Game over, lobster,' says Martin.

'Son, I'm sorry.'

'S'all right Da.' He knows I'm not talking about the lobster.

Sometimes I think I can't make a living any more, I can't support
my family. I should give it up, try my hand at something else. Other
times I think, nah, that's just me being a miserable git, we're gonnae
be all right. Look at this place. The stone pier, the sea, the foam
necklacing the shore. There are still plenty of lobsters out there, smelling
their way to my creels. They'll be at their night-walking tonight. Take
it from one who knows.

Palma McKeown

HOW TO BE SCOTS-ITALIAN

Get a head start by having a first name
that doesn't really go with your second name.
Your parents were just trying to keep everyone happy.
Keep a bottle of *Lacryma Christi* for when
your Auntie Anna calls in unexpectedly.
Hide the jar of instant coffee in case
she comes into the kitchen and dust off
the old metal coffee pot that unscrews in the middle.
Put out that *panettone* you got at Christmas
then watch as she scoffs all the Tunnock's Teacakes.
Learn to sidle down side streets or
melt into shop doorways when you see
old Mr D'Ambrosio coming because, despite
the fact he's lived here for over sixty years,
you still can't make out a word he's saying.
Be prepared to serve sausage rolls and *salami di Milano*
at Hogmanay parties and give equal play time
to Jimmy Shand and Dean Martin.
You're just trying to keep everyone happy.
Listen politely to your Auntie Carmen from Coatbridge
when she phones at three in the morning to ask
if everything's okay because she's had a dream
about you and the number 62
which signifies death and pestilence.
Try unsuccessfully to get back to sleep.
Feel torn when Italy is playing Scotland at football
until the crowd starts to sing 'Flower of Scotland'
and a wee tear runs down your cheek.
Try not to get bitter that you never knew
your Italian granddad because during the war

he was taken away by two Scottish policemen
in the middle of the night, herded onto a ship
and was lost at sea when it was torpedoed.
Churchill was just trying to keep everyone happy.

Ann MacKinnon

THE WINTER VISITOR

The pheasant appeared in the days
when winter was wet and grey. Red wattle
and bottle-green head declaring his arrival.

Somehow those barred green feathers
gave us hope as he bounded across the lawn,
ignoring lesser birds and sharp-clawed cats.

His colourful outfit demanded an occasion.
Seemingly tame, he tilted his head and stared
as we scattered seeds to hold him to us.

He waited until we turned away before eating,
then wiped the grass clean with gusto.
His head lifted, giving a nod of thanks.

We got through Christmas with his help.
When there were no words we fed him
and watched as he pecked up hope.

Now in March, he's still here,
preparing for better times
as he bursts upwards roaring his cry.

Olivia McMahon

THE JOURNEY

He said he could get there by train by changing twice –
at Edinburgh and Preston. Another route involved
three changes, one at the border town of Carlyle.
But there was a third way going by Glasgow
that he preferred, though it meant a change of station.
He liked the swoop of the west coast line. And then
the boat – a starry crossing. Or the shorter day crossing
with a stay in Liverpool. No, he'd go by night,
sail up the Liffey in the early morning,
the whole journey taking no more than a day
and a night. And I'm about to point out
that a plane would take not much more than an hour
when I've a change of heart: I dismiss my case.
Why has it taken me so long to reach this place?

Hugh McMillan

SETTLEMENT

I spend a lot of time in the hills
but there are always sheep above me,
hanging in space on their stilt legs,
or at the very edge of my vision
circling crags like small clouds.

When the mountains crumble
into the new age of seas,
they will survive,
they will bump along the ocean floor
with blank expressions

chewing seaweed,
their lambs coming and going
quickly, like fish.
It will be a mystery how this will happen
but it will:

those with a bit of brain,
seeing the absurdity of their situation,
will drown, but the vast crowd,
having no doubts of their own,
will take it as read.

Marion F. Morrison

MÀIRI À MAGDALA, NA H-AONAR LE
A SMUAINTEAN

Bha dròbhan dhiubh air cladaichean Ghalilee
Gràisg na sgothan iasgaich,
'S an cuid siol a' fannachadh leis an acras
Beòil fosgailte
Sùilean dall.

Is tusa led threud
Ag èalaidh gu tìr
Falamh.
Na beathaichean acrach, air an clisgeadh,
Na marsantan a' gearan 's a' caitheamh smugaidean
'S gam sgrùdadh gu drùiseach

Air dhut do ghàirdeanan fhosgladh,
Bhiadhadh iad agus dh'fhàs iad socair.
Am measg an t-sluaigh
Sheas thu
Fada os cionn chàich.
Fada nad bharail fhèin – a rèir choltais.
Bha brunndail a' dol
Is fathannan a' dol mun cuairt
A dh'aindeoin do shùilean bàidheil
A' glaodhaich,
'Bi timcheall orm
Bheir urram dhomh
Thoir gaol dhomh.'

Cho luath 's a mhothaich thu dhomhsa
Bha thu aig mo dhoras
Cha b' e ruith ach leum
Agus bha iad mionnaichte

Gun robh sinn còmhla
Ann an gaol.
(Leig mi leotha.)
Thadhail thu orm gun teagamh.
Ach cha b' ann 'son pòg sgreamhail,
A' bhàis bhig.
Dh'ung mi thu le ola
Ach cha deach ar cridheachan thairis.

Ann am priobadh na sùla
Bha thu mar uirsgeul
Cha do dh'amharc mi air do chràdh neo air na dh'fhuiling thu.
Do bhàs.
Na boireannaich a' sgiamhail
Dhubh mi às iad
Làn prois gun robh mo chridhe fhèin
A' cumail a-mach às.
Ach – gun fhiosta – thill thu, thugamsa
Dìreach aon turas
Mar chomharradh air an deireadh ùr.

Ach bho àm gu àm
Air cladaichean Tabgha
Bidh thu tighinn fainear dhomh
Aig dol fodha na grèine
Am measg na reultan aognaidh
A' chraobh bhàn-dhearg almon
'S a blàthan cùbhraidh
A' cur an fhìrinn eagalach ma sgaoil.

MARY OF MAGDALA BY HERSELF

The shores of Galilee awash with them.
All starved, those foul fisher folk
With their spawn. Mouths agape.
Eyes blank.
And you with your raggedy band sliding ashore
Empty to the gunnels.
The merchants
With their beasts hungry and nervous
Muttered and spat,
Rolling their eyes over me in leering speculation.

In the spreading of your arms somehow they were fed and
          quietened.
Your height alone quelled them as you stood head and shoulders
On the hillside
Above the rest.
Above yourself – some said.
There was already muttering
Despite your eloquent eyes
Pleading,
'Know me.
Praise me.
Love me.'

One penetrating look
And you were soon at my door
And famously they said we 'shared a love'.
(I let it stick.)
And yes you did call on me,
But not for us the reechy kiss
The little death.
I anointed you with oil

But our hearts
Did not run over.

Before I knew it
You were past tense.
I did not watch the death throes.
I shut out the *ululantes*
Quite proud of my own heart
Beating a retreat.
And then you were back – just once to me
Like a consummation of a new ending.

Sometimes on the shore at Tabgha
I catch you in the sun setting.
Just to a pinpoint
Among the bleak stars
And gaze upon the pink almond tree
Scenting the cruel truth.

Danny Murphy

CRAWFORD

The low grey cottages on Shottsmuir had been built before the first war for the families of shepherds, but there were no shepherds now. The windows of the one on the right had been boarded over but one of the boards was working itself loose in the wind, banging and banging against the frame. A boy of about fifteen came out the door of the other cottage, walked round and started to pull at the loose board. He was followed by a small wiry woman.

'Crawford,' she shouted. 'Where's your schoolbag that I got you?'

Crawford yanked at the plank, then looked round. 'Ah dinny need a bag the day.'

'You need a bag every day,' she said.

He wrenched the plank free, threw it away then turned to face her. He was dressed all in black – his version of the Benhar Academy uniform. Steel-toed workboots, denim, a shapeless work-jacket, short-cropped black hair. This was him now, home with his mother.

'Ah dinny need a bag the day,' he repeated.

Beneath the wind, they both heard the school bus toiling up the brae. They watched it go past and reverse in, ready to pick him up. Crawford inhaled the diesel fumes.

It was late August. The driver had been forced to make this extra journey up to the cottage now Crawford was back from his secure placement at Kerebell School. First day in, he'd let Crawford know he didn't appreciate having to drive out here. 'It'll be worse in the winter,' he'd said. They hadn't spoken since. Crawford boarded the bus and sat in a back corner. As the bus pulled away, he turned away from his mother and bit his grimy nails.

Next stop was Shottsmuir Farm, a half-mile or so down the road, where a gaggle of wee girls waited. They knew not to sit near him. Wee Michael got on at the next road end. Michael was a wee tube but Crawford liked him and his toothy grin. He was a talker all right.

'Whit yi been up tae, yi wee wide-o?'

'Ah wis away wi my da at the weekend. Doon at the merket at Longtoon. We took a load uv sheep doon. There's this guy there, Loppy they cry him. He's got the most amazin ears man. Pure mental. They're massive, like a dug's ears. He's an old guy, like . . .'

Crawford looked round. 'Whose sheep?'

'How do ah know whose sheep? We went doon to somewhere near Lanark. Pure early man. Ah wis away afore five on Seterday. The farmer had this cute wee dug, a collie, beauty, ah wouldnie mind a dug like that. He's cried "Brave", somehin like that. Ah'd to help clean oot the lorry when we goat back.' Michael could talk on. It kept the journey going. More wee kids, wet coats and wet schoolbags steaming up the windows.

Outside school there was the usual melee as the buses arrived from all quarters round. Farms, former mining villages, the big new estate backing onto the motorway. Crawford and Michael headed for the back of the games hall for a fag. The rain had stopped. Michael offered Crawford one then lit his own, taking in the first drag with a flourish.

'So whit were yi up to at the weekend man? Did yi get any rabbits?' he asked.

Crawford took a long draw, looking down at his fag as he blew the smoke out. 'Aye. Ah wis up the woods wi ma airgun and ma dug. Ah did awright.'

'Ah luv yir dug man. But ah'm scared o it since that time, ken, when ah came roon fir yi an it went fir us.' Crawford laughed. 'It wisnae funny man, ah nearly shat ma breeks. Oh-oh . . .'

They'd both seen wee Goagsy'd poke his head round the side of the games hall, then run off when he spotted them.

'See that?' Crawford said.

'Aye.'

'Well see if Brannie comes, you git tae fuck, Michael,' Crawford said. 'This isnae your battle.'

'Aye, but . . .' Michael's voice tailed away.

A small gang of maybe ten boys appeared from round the corner and stopped a few yards away. Goagsy was in there, but it was big prick Tam Brannie that was the man. Crawford knew it for what it was. The same shit every place he went.

He turned to Michael. 'Go on. Git.' Michael moved away into the crowd which was gathering round to watch the action. Crawford stayed where he was and took another drag, eyeing the gang indifferently, his fag held between finger and thumb.

'What the fuck'r you looking at, ferm boy?' It was Tam. Crawford eyed him up, his Lacoste jacket, his Loakes brogues.

'Ah'm no lookin at nothin.' It was a neutral statement, but Tam didn't want neutral.

'Ah heard that yi'd said yi cid take anywan in this school. Is that right?'

'Ah'm no lookin to take no-one.'

The crowd was pressing round closer. Tam was working himself up.

'Jist cos yir the big boy goat sent aff tae Kerebell an yir da's in the Bar-L. Think yi can take anywan eh?'

'Ah nivir said that.'

'Well take it back then.'

Crawford finished his fag and stubbed it out on the slab. He looked at Tam. 'Ah'm arney takin back whit ah nivir said.'

Tam squared his shoulders and looked round at his team. 'Well we say yi huvtie.'

This time Crawford measured his voice out. 'An ah say that ah dinny give a flyin fuck whit youse say.'

Just at that the bell went.

Tam moved towards Crawford. 'That's no very nice, is it? Eh? Yir gonnie huvtie back that up, ferm boy. Eh?'

A loud voice was heard from behind the crowd. It was Mr Manson. 'What's going on here? Break this up!'

'Dennertime. Doon the muir,' Tam said, then turned round to face the Depute Head.

'What's going on here, Thomas?'

'It's nothin sur. We wiz aw jist havin a wee chat n that, eh?'

Mr Manson looked round. 'Well don't just stand there.' He waved his arms. 'Get off to your tutor groups. The bell went five minutes ago.'

'Sur, it was actually jist two minutes ago,' Goagsy said, grinning, and ran away.

Crawford waited till the others had moved off. Only he and Manson were left.

'You're the boy who came to us from Kerebell last week, aren't you?'
Manson asked.

Crawford nodded.

'Well don't get yourself into any trouble here. If there's a problem
with any of the other boys, just come and tell us.'

*

By the time it got to lunchtime, Crawford knew there was no way
out. In Science, things had been said round the desk. It was about
time someone stuck one on big Tam. He was a shitebag. Just cos he
came from Clyde, he thought he was harder than anyone else. In the
corridor on the way to PSE, wee guys he didn't know were coming
up to him: 'Ur yi gonnie fight him?' 'You can take him easy.' 'Good
luck, big man.' In PSE, wee Goagsy'd kept right away from him, the
wee crapper.

After the lunch bell, Crawford went to the toilet, then glanced through
the dining hall window as he left the school building. Manson was
caught up in there, a crowd of first years round him. By the time
Crawford'd climbed over the corner fence and got down to the town
muir through the wee wood, it seemed like half the school was there.
The fight was going ahead all right. The crowd parted and Crawford
walked through to the central arena. Big Tam was pacing around,
psyching himself up. When he saw Crawford, he shouted at him.

'Right yi bastard, yir fir it noo.'

'Aye, mebbie, but no fae a shitebag likesay you, yi lardy cunt.'

At that, Tam whipped out a length of bike chain and lashed it at
Crawford's head. Crawford ducked and deflected it off his wrist. It
deadened his arm and he staggered back. Tam pressed forward and
swung the chain again, but Crawford had stumbled backwards and
fallen against the crowd. Tam was unbalanced by the force he'd put
into swinging the chain and staggered slightly to the side on one foot.
Lying on his back, Crawford caught Tam's right ankle between his feet
and twisted him over. As Tam fell, the chain underneath him, Crawford
sprang up and stood astride him, pinning his right wrist with his left
foot. Tam grabbed at Crawford's leg with his other hand, but Crawford

brought the heel of his right boot down on his cheek with a crunching sound. Tam was squirming but couldn't get his arm free. The chain was useless. He grabbed Crawford's other leg and tried to unbalance him, to pull him down, but he was too stable. They were stalemated. Crawford flexed the fingers of his left hand. He looked down at Tam.

'Ah nivir wanted tae fight yi but seein as ah am, yir gonnie get the doin uv yir miserable cunty life.'

Tam stretched for the chain with his free hand but Crawford was ahead of him and had a hold of it already. As Tam tried to get up and at the same time to wrestle the chain free, Crawford caught him with a punch to his temple that knocked him back. Tam loosened his grip and Crawford pulled the chain from his hand and threw it away, then as Tam came up a second time Crawford caught him on the chin with his boot. Tam fell back. Crawford knelt astride him and pummelled him with his right fist. The crowd groaned.

Crawford stood up and swept them with such a look that those in the front row pushed back and one or two fell over onto those behind them. Tam was trying to get up. Crawford caught him again, this time with the left boot. Then he stooped over and picked up Tam's hand.

'See this?' he said. 'This is whit youse get if yi mess wi me.' He took Tam's right index finger and bent it back till there was a crack. Tam screamed in pain. Crawford lined up another kick to his head, but looked up, looked round, and walked away. The crowd quickly began to drift back to school, leaving Tam lying in the field, Goagsy and a few others round him.

As he strolled back to school, a small crowd of acolytes surrounded Crawford. 'That wiz pure brilliant, man.' 'Did yi see the way Tam went ower?' 'That wiz right ootie order, bringin his chain an that eh but Crawford saw it comin.' 'He deserved whit he goat, the big cunt.' 'He's been askin fir it eh?' 'Well done Crawford. You're the man noo.'

Back in the school grounds, Crawford examined his bruised knuckles.

'You better watch yourself, Crawford,' Charmaine told him. 'That Tam's got loadsuv cousins an that up in Clyde. They'll come eftir you.'

'They're aw shitebags like him. Bring them oan.' He was still on fire, remembering each move, each detail.

*

Next period was Music. Crawford was playing drums in a little group that was preparing a number for a show. The girl singer came on to him as she handed him his drumsticks. 'Can you play all right, Crawford?'

He looked at her. 'Ah cin play,' he said.

Mr Manson appeared at the door soon enough. Crawford followed him up the corridor, listening to Manson's shoes squeaking on the polished floor, watching the turn-ups on his suit trousers flapping around his ankles.

'Crawford,' he began once they were sitting in his office, 'lots of people are telling me that you assaulted Tom Brannie down the muir at lunchtime. I've had to send him to hospital. This could be very serious. I want you to tell me exactly what happened and I'll write it down.'

Crawford looked out of the window.

'Or if you prefer you can answer my questions.'

Crawford half shrugged.

'Well, how did this start?'

'Brannie's an eejit, eh? He's been in ma face since ah started last week. Him and his wee mates. Ah didnie wanna fight but ah dinny have a choice cos he's set it up that wye. When ah gets ben the muir, he's at me wi his bike chain. Big man eh? Needs a chain. So ah takes it aff him and ah does him. That's it.'

'Someone told me you'd deliberately broken his finger. Is that right?'

'Naw, naw. If his finger got broke, it's aw part o the same thing eh? Ah gave as good as ah goat. That's all. He attacked me wi a chain, mind. That's aw there is aboot it.'

'But I was told you dispossessed him of the chain. You could have left it at that.'

For the first time Crawford looked straight at Manson. A hesitant, balding man in his late fifties. Somebody had said he was a good Maths teacher. Crawford looked away again and spoke more slowly, pronouncing each syllable exactly, as if Manson was the child.

'When someone attacks you wi a bike chain, you don't take it aff them and walk away.'

Manson said nothing but kept writing for a bit more. Crawford looked out the window. Across the rooftops, he could see the open moorland.

'Well I'll have to speak to Mrs McGowan, Crawford, and see what she says about all this. It could be very serious; after all, you've only just started here. You've really let all of us down, especially Mrs McGowan. I know she was very keen that you were given every chance to make a fresh start here. Have you anything else to say?'

They could both hear the clattering of cutlery as the dinner ladies finished clearing up.

'Well if you've nothing more to say, can you read what I've written here and then sign at the bottom to say that it's an accurate record of what you told me?'

Crawford signed and put the pen in his pocket.

'Now I'll have to keep you out of circulation till Mrs McGowan gets back. When she does, we'll see what's to happen next. I'm going to put you in one of the interview rooms beside her office. All right?'

Crawford was in the interview room for the rest of the afternoon. He picked up the school brochure that was sitting on the table. 'A message from Mrs McGowan. Benhar Academy aims to get the best from every child . . .' He flicked through the pages. 'Our skiing trip to Aosta by Cheryl Lambert.' 'Photos of the school production of *Annie Get Your Gun.*' 'School teams. S3 football,' he read, 'back row T. Brannie.' He tore out the page, crumpled it up and threw it in the bin. Time passed. He read the notices on the wall. Fire drill procedure. Wash your hands. Switch off the lights. One of the desks had been sanded but you could still read what had been written on it. FTP. 1D. RFC. He added his initials with Manson's pen. CFC. Yeah. That was him. Crawford Finn Calder. One of the Bhoys.

It was a long afternoon.

He didn't see Mrs McGowan after all. Mr Manson escorted him down to the bus at the end of the day and explained that she was tied up in interviews for a new teaching post. 'I'm going to phone your mother tonight. We'll need to sort out what's to happen next,' he said. 'When does she get in from work?'

'It depends. Six or seven.'

'Well tell her I'm going to phone her then.'

When Crawford got back to the cottage, Boney, his Dobermann/
retriever cross, was pining for him. They went out into the high field.
He and Boney ran free till they were exhausted. Then they sat close
together in the wind. Crawford put his arm round the dog. Together,
they watched his mother's beat-up red Corsa edge its way along the
tiny road far below.

Donald S. Murray

POLISH SONGS OVERHEARD AT THE HYDRO DAM

Not of *Peigi Bhan* nor *Roisin Dhubh* nor any girl they loved
nor of boats to Carrickfergus, Stornoway, Ballyjamesduff
but the wads within their wallets when they were at last paid off.

Not of Uig's beaches nor of Gweedore's sands
nor the chant of prayer or rosary nor the swell and fall of psalms
but the knowledge there was more than muck that still clung to
    their hands.

Not the embrace of a mother nor a father's restrained smile
nor the neighbour's cheerful question – *'Are you with us for
    a while?'*
but the coldness of that pale sun witnessed in exile.

Not of heather, shamrock nor of need for the Auld Sod
nor the faith in Jesus lost in Highland rain and fog
but the thought of fields they once ploughed, fertilised by their
    friends' blood,

And that agony of absence for which glass brings no relief,
the knowledge that your homeland has been stolen, seized,
the bones of lost relations, the grime and grit and grief.

TRADITIONS

The dust of silver ferns upon soiled fingers,
the red slash of an iris, scarlet rose:
I watch these migrant workers shuffling across Lincolnshire,
plucking bouquets out for lovers from these fields where
      they grow

and flourish in abundance. They remind me, too, of those
of my people who sailed south for endless hours
to coat their hands in silver, cut palms and fingers, too,
with the knives they held within their clutch, wounds crimson
      as these flowers.

Stephen Nelson

ALL ABOUT ARLENE

My first months of love! Remembering
Arlene's shorts, terry towelling, with yellow trim,
the smell of her bedroom and her curious little sister;
her teacher nearby, an all-seeing eye, yet casual, strangely
      benevolent.
Sitting silently with Arlene, how she gave me a football sticker,
her scent clinging to the card, then ran shyly away,
before I could tell her how much I liked it.
How she walked like a cheetah, and ran like a deer,
an elegant huntress imagining cubs beyond the threshold
of girlhood.
And her friend, with the haunted house on the corner. Walking
      home with her friend.
Picturing the pink Valentine she sent me, hearts drawn in
      crayon,
and again her scent, that musk, her essence in scent.
The Postie rhyme. The roses rhyme.
Be my funny Valentine.
Then the emptiness of the scheme when she disappeared and I
      didn't know why;
why she left me, and the sad song John Travolta sang in *Grease*,
the sad song about Sandy, why she left him, why-y-y oh why,
      you left me, oh Sandy . . .
Why . . .

. . . seeing her thirty years later, walking like a deer past the
      coffee shop,
knowing the blue wheel of destiny, the intensity of an encounter
with the incomprehensible innocence of childhood;
dreaming dreams which reconcile the intervening years,
dreams of the underworld, of descent; the retrieval of a
      broken stone . . .

why seeing her now is a pillar of light in an interconnected web
of primal, dancing energy, a sparkling periwinkle waltz.
Why seeing her now affects so much, is vital, crucial, ecstatic.

Watching Arlene on a bike, smiling, her skinny legs kicking,
    where loss
is an unforeseeable panther lurking in the hedges,
and I am not quite the lion I think I am.
And who knows, if I had returned the Valentine
instead of drowning in puddles of rain on the way home
    from school,
the world might have remained innocent and incomplete,
trapped in unknowing for centuries,
while the new earth watches its body drift around
imaginary suns, like a bedazzled actress, whose blazing star
forgot to rise.

Niall O'Gallagher

'GHILLE BHIG . . .'

Ghille bhig
cha bu tric
a rinn mis'
    leithid gàir'

gus an robh
thus' an seo
cha b' eòl dhomh
    briseadh là

's tu, a leig
iolach bheag
falach-fead
    air mo sgàth,

na do dhùisg
casan rùisgt'
madainn ùr
    sa mhoch-thràith.

B. D. Owens

HOME COMING

My father talks slow now.
No longer the power-wielding jester,
always cutting, always seizing the centre of things.

A flat, weak, but kinder version slumps before me.
Searching eyes, desperate for knowing,
but constrained by lingering arrogance,
which will inevitably stake out the lines,
of censorship and denial.

It has taken me nineteen years to return.
The prodigal son?
No, I won't give him that,
but I won't give him the queer truth either.
He does not deserve truth.
He has lived his own continuous lie,
shaped by desire and shame,
forged by fear-laced hatred.

An impasse.
How does one proceed?
Like always.
With pity, with armour, with grace.

Chris Powici

THE WILD SUMMER

i.m. Angus Dunn

Nights and days of blinding rain, Atlantic lows
sweeping across the carse
trees and hills lost in thick noonday mist.

Now this raw light
and a hard Steppe wind pouring down Glen Tye
towards the late sun.

A raven lifts from a fencepost
and gives itself to the cold, marvellous air
pitching and wheeling
as if there's no tomorrow, as if there's
only ever hunger, longing, flight – here, now

and this, as you know, is the real poem Angus –
a lone dark bird telling the truth about the world
telling it well –
not these words

though, given time, I'll get them as right as I can
even if there's no raven, just skeins of autumn greylag
flowing calmly south.

Even if it's way too late by then.

Stewart Sanderson

SIR LEONARD WOOLLEY, UR

Our master Caesar is in the tent . . .

Once, these were Lady Puabi's jewels –
carnelian and lapis, glimmering
like little planets in the dark welkin
of her coiffure; inwoven flowerets
mimicked with golden foil. I lay them out
spreading them evenly over the off-
white cotton tablecloth. Outside my tent
night sounds – a dog's yelp, muttered Arabic,
a desert sigh: wind sifting emptiness.
Inside, lamplight trembles. I lay them out
grouping by size, by style, material;
above all, where we found them. So her maids
arranged them for her once, lifting each bauble
from its cedar box and setting it before
her on the dresser. Yes, it is as though
I reached out through the flysheet and felt soft
brown fingers brush on mine. I lay them out
considering Lady Puabi's smile
at some figment of court gossip; her frown
faced with momentary embarrassment
to her faction. Under the thought, her skull
crushed flat by earth, grins, packed in newspaper
a tent or two away. I lay them out
wondering if she died a dowager
or an infanta. Was she Rosalind
quipping in Arden, or Ophelia
wallowing downstream? Gertrude perhaps
comes nearest to her end, or Cleopatra
catching Antonies. I lay them out
dreaming on headlines – *Human Sacrifice
at Ur*; *Exclusive: Pit of Death Discovered* . . .

Just yellow paper in a week. Enough
to set a fire or poke the Honours List
but nothing to the mystery of this
woman her servants followed willingly
into the ground. Her jewels. I lay them out
imagining that all this tarnished gleam
were mine. It goes with her to Bloomsbury.

Caroline von Schmalensee

MAKIRUKU'S FIRST COURTSHIP

'Mine was one of thirty-five eggs,' Makiruku said with a satisfied grin, 'but only I survived. It was my mother's first clutch, you see, and she dug too close to the water. The burrow flooded. The shells on the eggs softened. My siblings rotted.'

His audience gasped. In rotting clutches, the bottom layer of eggs collapsed and the corruption spread upwards, the pile of eggs forming a kind of sponge, sucking a noxious mess of salt water and decomposing clutchlings up into itself.

No one survived.

The listeners stared at Makiruku in awe. He sunned himself in their attention, combing his dark green hair over a dark mahogany forehead.

*

Back then, when Makiruku was still in his home town, he earned his supper telling stories. Some of them were true, many were not. The one about his birth was.

*

'The first thing I remember is light,' he said, squinting towards the sun and holding his hands up to simulate a crack in an eggshell. 'Is it the first thing you remember too?' He'd throw his arms wide as if to embrace everyone listening. On a busy market day, that could be a couple of dozen kappa. This was a slow day, and there were only a few clutchlings and their keepers nodding their answer to his question.

And a blue-shelled girl was there. It was the first time he saw her.

*

'What's the second thing you remember?' he asked the clutchling sitting next to the blue girl. Makiruku was good at telling who would give a good answer. He'd spot the open beak and the glazed eyes that showed someone walking the memory road. The answer would vary, but was usually 'the smell of salt water', or 'the sound of the sea'.

'The smell of the sea,' the clutchling said shyly. Makiruku nodded. 'That's not what I remember,' he said. He crouched as if still inside the egg. Tapping an imaginary shell with his beak, and pushing at it with his hands, he mimed sticking his head out into the world. He took a deep breath and screwed his face up in disgust.

'Death,' he said, 'that's the second thing I remember. The stench of death thick around me. The sound of death coming towards me as the eggs below cracked and crunched from my struggle. The movement of death as the shell I was still in slewed to the side.' He twisted sharply to the right and froze, precariously perched on one leg.

Everyone remembered clambering out of their own egg: the fear when their world changed, the confusion as they crawled into cool darkness instead of warm light, the frantic scrabble to the surface of the burrow. Some remembered clambering over glassy eggs, others, who hatched later, remembered sharp edges and siblings kicking sand into their eyes.

'The burrow was almost completely filled with water,' Makiruku continued. 'I got out of the shell, but the surface was receding, the light a mere suggestion up above. Water and slime covered my legs, bits of bone and shell stabbed my still-soft chest plate.'

He paused and let everyone feel the awfulness of his situation. He gazed at the blue kappa. She looked troubled. He'd hoped for horrified.

'I wanted to live, but my siblings wanted me with them.' He mimed falling away from the sun and the surface, one arm outstretched, his beak open in a silent scream.

*

In those days, Makiruku was a handsome youth. His black eyes glittered with humour and his shell had a deep burgundy gloss, like good lacquer. His limbs were straight and strong. At the top of his head, in the indentation his kind call their head-bowl, his spirit liquor glistened. This was a long time before he became the twisted creature he is now, before his head-bowl was washed clean and he lost his strength. Long before his shell deformed and pushed his head into his chest, his arms out in front of him.

In the market he still thought highly of himself, and so did the people who listened to him.

*

'I strove for the light,' he said. 'I kicked with my legs and grasped with my hands. Something caught one foot.' He stood frozen, leg stretched behind him.

'My whole shell was submerged in sibling sludge.' He shook his leg violently. 'But I kicked again, I panted and fought and with a last effort I pulled myself out of the midden the burrow had become. My mother greeted me with a rain of tears. "Where are the others?" she wailed, clutching my slimy, stinking body to her chest. "Where are your siblings?"'

*

This part of the story was not true. Makiruku's mother had been so appalled by the state of her one surviving offspring and so embarrassed about her incompetent burrowing that she ran away and hid in the forest for three days. It was her sister who cleaned and fed him. She'd been waiting for her clutch nearby. 'What's one more?' she'd said when Makiruku's mother returned for her boy. 'Thirty or thirty-one – it makes no difference.' It was her fifth clutch: she was an experienced mother.

*

Makiruku pressed a pretend child to his heart and looked at it with sorrowful eyes. His long eyelashes threw shadows on his cheeks. He held the silence for a couple of seconds.

'Then a smile graced her lips and she kissed me.' He smiled. '"You are the most precious gift," she said and took me home, boasting to her neighbours of my persistence and strength.'

He stood up straight, showing his full length, before making a graceful curtsey. He held the gaze of the blue girl as he bent his legs.

The little group applauded. Some of the young ones asked for another story but the one he was interested in got up and walked away. Makiruku gazed after her. She had something special. It was more than the blue shell, something in how she held herself.

That evening, as Makiruku caught up the trinkets and foodstuffs the people of the market had given him in exchange for his stories, he thought about having someone by his side when he worked. Not his mother, who didn't come to watch him very often any more, but another adoring someone. A companion and admirer. Someone who would make others respect him all the more for having her. Someone beautiful like the girl who had listened to him that morning.

The idea took root as he walked home and when he sat down to supper he told his mother, 'I have found the kappa I will marry.'

His mother put a bowl of sea cucumbers and seaweed in front of him and poured herself a cup of tea. It was a gentle night, so they sat at the table on the back porch. The night air was scented with herbs and as soft as the wood under their hands.

'How lovely. Do I know her?'

'No,' Makiruku said, tucking in. 'And neither do I. I need your help to discover who she is.'

'My help, indeed,' said Makiruku's mother and curled her hands around her cup in a way that would have told her other children that she was tired of helping and wished to be left alone to tend her house and wait for her husband's occasional visits. She loved her first-hatched but she had expected him to move out by now. The guilt over his hatching had never left her, but it was getting increasingly tiresome to carry. She'd had six clutches after that first disastrous one. At one point, she'd had ninety little ones living at home. The older clutches helped care for the younger but it was still hard work.

*

Bringing up young brought almost as much heartbreak as it did pleasure. She'd lost twelve hatchlings to birds of prey, eight to humans who thought they were malformed sea turtles, six to sharks, five to dogs, three to cats and one, in a bizarre and bloody accident, to purple crabs. But she'd kept most of them alive, to thrive and move out at five years old, as kappa should. The village was full of her offspring, some with homes of their own, some living in the singles house, where Makiruku too should be.

Her sister went to sea after bringing up her eighth clutch. Makiruku's mother wanted to stay on land. She didn't fancy roaming the seas to get solitude, or living in a pond, giving humans cryptic advice in exchange for morsels of food. She just wanted peace.

'So what does she look like, this wife-to-be of yours?' she asked.

Makiruku slurped the last of his seaweed and pushed his bowl aside.

'Her shell is blue,' he said, unfocusing his eyes the better to recall her. 'Her hair is black, like her eyes, and her arms have a blue tint. I think even her shadow is blue. She walks very straight. I have never seen anyone like her.' He pulled his gaze back to the here and now. Snapping his beak playfully at his mother he said, 'She saw me tell a tale today, so she's probably already half in love with me.'

'No doubt,' said his mother. 'If so, she'll come back tomorrow. Or the day after.' She sighed and dipped a claw in her tea. A couple of drops of tea clung to her nail. She transferred them to her head-bowl to soften the liquid. She needed to think.

'I'll come with you tomorrow,' she said, 'and walk the market. Maybe I can find out who she is.'

*

Makiruku's mother had many friends in the market so it didn't take her long to find out all about his intended. Emiko was from the third clutch of one of their neighbour Taani's clutch-sister's fourth-clutch daughters. She'd come to visit the village and have a look at the singles house. She was Makiruku's age, more or less, and a hard worker.

Makiruku's mother kept this information to herself. She wanted to meet Emiko before sharing gossip with her son and she wanted to know if her son was serious. She needed to see the two together. But Emiko didn't come that day, or even the next. So for the weeks that followed, his mother shadowed Makiruku in the market.

*

It was a month before Makiruku saw his love again. He sometimes thought he glimpsed the blue of her shell in the crowds but she didn't sit down to listen to him.

When she finally did, he told a story of chivalry and romance, and singled her out to tell the story to, to show that he'd noticed her. He thought he caught a slight flush on her cheeks when he finished and read it as delight at his attention. Like the first time, she left after only one story.

'She's so shy,' thought Makiruku, 'so demure.'

*

Makiruku's mother watched her son do his act and noticed the young kappa he desired. Her son made a fool of himself but the girl behaved well. After the performance, she tapped Emiko's shell before she could disappear into the crowd.

'Here,' she said and stretched out a hand for touching, 'you're Emiko, aren't you?'

'I am,' Emiko said and brushed her soft light-blue hand over the older kappa's brown, wrinkled paw. Makiruku's mother enjoyed the touch. She liked her own hands, pads calloused from collecting seaweed to feed her family, and from scrubbing the cedar-wood porch that wrapped around her house. Her hands showed the signs of a good life and she kept her black claws neat. Emiko's hand belonged to someone who still had a life to live. Her nails were opalescent in the sunlight, her skin thin and delicate, her pads soft and warm.

'I'm Kame,' said Makiruku's mother. 'I know your mother's sibling Taani. She's told me about you. Let me buy you a cup of tea.' She smiled. 'If you have time?'

Emiko nodded and smiled her assent.

Kame took a light hold of the edge of Emiko's shell and led her to a tea house. She could understand her son's interest in this girl. The shell she held was soft and smooth, as if polished by a master lacquer-maker. Its ridges were highlighted in sky blue, the valleys between a deep indigo. It smelled pleasantly of warm bone where Kame had expected it to reek of beeswax. Emiko's chest plate was blue too, flecked with red and gold, not the pedestrian cream Makiruku and his mother shared. The gloss would fade but the colours would always be startling. Kame smiled and caressed Emiko's shell as they waited for the tea things to be brought.

'Indulge an old lady,' she said and laughed at her own boldness. 'I am amazed at how lustrous your shell is. It reminds me of a story a friend of mine told me when we were young. She was recently married and her husband would come home at night and "polish her shell". We'd always thought the expression a euphemism but, no, not for him. He had a cloth and a pot of flower-scented wax and polished and polished and polished. She gleamed.'

Emiko laughed. 'It's the colour,' she said, 'my sisters are as bright.' Her spirit liquor glittered in her merriment.

Kame busied herself with making tea. 'Taani tells me you're visiting from three villages down. What's the attraction?'

'Taani is my favourite relative,' Emiko said, 'and I hear there's room in your singles house. Ours is full – the last few seasons' clutches have been very successful.'

Kame nodded. 'We've had bad weather,' she said.

'So I understand.'

'And moles,' Kame said.

Emiko shivered. Moles could take out an entire beach of clutches; digging, crushing, letting water into and heat out of burrows.

'But why the singles house? Why not look for a husband? With colour like yours you must have admirers everywhere.'

Emiko blushed. They sipped the tea Kame had poured.

'I don't know,' she said. 'I've never met anyone I want to spend time with in that way. I like to work and be free.'

'Are you finding work?'

'I am. I help with the kelp harvest and I collect mussels.'

Kame approved. Those were good jobs. Hard but not dangerous work that prepared you for looking after your own clutch one day.

'Do you have friends here?'

'Only Taani, so far. And now you, I hope.' Emiko looked at Kame from under lowered lashes. Then she grimaced. 'I'm not good at making friends.'

'Would you not like to meet someone your own age?'

Emiko shook her head. 'I'm quite happy as I am.'

*

'It's not going to happen, son,' Makiruku's mother told him over dinner a few days later. She was watching Makiruku crunch seaweed, a blend of robust kelp given her by Emiko when they'd met for tea again that morning, and more gentle species she grew in her own water beds. She'd scented it with crushed sesame seeds.

Makiruku stared. He chewed furiously and swallowed. 'What isn't?' he asked.

'Emiko. That's the name of your young blue love. I told you I'd find out. You won't win her.' She sighed. She liked the girl. She was polite, self-sufficient, hard-working and pretty too.

'Why not?' Makiruku was aghast. His little black eyes bulged, his jaws worked. A drop of algae green spittle fell from the tip of his beak into his bowl. He banged his hands on the table. Kame sighed again.

'She's not interested.'

'But she's seen me tell stories,' Makiruku said. 'Twice!'

'She's happy as she is.'

'But I love her.'

Makiruku and his mother looked at each other. Kame shrugged.

'I told one of the stories directly to her. It was a dedication, a public love letter. She can't ignore that.'

'You loving her doesn't oblige her to love you, Makiruku.'

'Of course it does. Otherwise I'm a fool, in love with a nameless stranger.'

'Loving is never foolish but expecting reciprocity is unwise.'

Makiruku threw his bowl with such force it sailed over the porch railing and into the garden, where it landed in a clump of irises. It didn't break. With a yelp of irritation Makiruku stormed off.

'That girl has to love me,' he yelled, 'she HAS to.'

Kame collected the thrown bowl.

'Emiko,' she said quietly, 'her name is Emiko. I told you.'

*

Makiruku's fame stems from this period. In an attempt to entice the unknown beauty back, Makiruku's stories became more outlandish and his performances more elaborate. He made many innovations. Every day, he had a new tale or a new prop. He started singing and using a cymbal. The crowds loved it: they had never experienced storytelling like it. These days, all Makiruku's tools are commonplace in market theatre, but then he was revolutionary.

*

Makiruku itched with dissatisfaction until the day Emiko joined the audience for a third time. He had practised for the event and had a story no one had heard before. It told of a lonely hero, the sole survivor of his clutch, a beautiful maiden and the hero's attempts to save her from a life of seaweed-growing drudgery. It started with a song and ended with a short dance in the interpretative style. The crowd gave him a standing ovation and called for the dance again.

Only Emiko didn't cheer. She left.

Makiruku gave up all his dreams of having her by his side. It was obvious to him that she was as heartless as her shell was shiny.

For three weeks he mourned his first love, telling nothing but stories of crushed dreams and thwarted ambitions, including a version of his own hatching story in which he died. He sprinkled his head with ash, turning hair and spirit liquor a murky grey. He moaned, recited funeral rhymes and crawled in the dust. Audiences thinned.

But he couldn't mourn for long. Soon he started telling happier stories. His new tales were about silly people who couldn't see what was in front of their eyes, or youngsters making decisions they'd come to regret. Humour softened any bitter edges. Makiruku continued to sing and to dance and the market crowds adored him anew.

*

Meanwhile, Kame and Emiko's friendship grew. When Makiruku was busy in the market, the two were often seen at Taani's, helping her weed her herb garden, or drinking tea at Kame's water beds.

'Do you know the storyteller?' Emiko asked Kame one day.

'In the market?'

'Yes, the one with the cymbal, he who dances.' She giggled.

'Yes,' said Kame, 'he's my son.'

'Oh,' said Emiko, her face going sombre.

They sat silent for a while.

'Imagine you didn't know,' said Kame. 'What were you going to say?'

Emiko laughed, a sound like ringing bluebells. 'I used to think he fancied me.'

Kame's laugh joined Emiko's. 'Oh,' she said, 'he really did.'

'But he didn't even speak to me,' Emiko laughed, 'just capered and told the strangest stories.'

'I love him,' said Kame, 'but he's not very good with social niceties. It was his first courtship.'

'I hope he does better next time.' Emiko raised her teacup to Kame, who patted her hand affectionately.

*

'Mine was one of thirty-five eggs,' Makiruku said, a sad frown furrowing his forehead, 'but only I survived.'

He turned his gaze on a gold-red girl sitting in the front row. This was the fourth story she'd stayed for. Her eyes were bright, her beak half open. She gleamed in the midday brightness. Makiruku raised his shell rattle and shook it, making the watery sound swell from gentle breakers to crashing waves.

He would make this girl fall in love with him. Then she'd come to the market every day without him having to marry her. He tried not to smile.

'It was my mother's first clutch, you see, and she dug too close to the water.'

Andrew Sclater

ORDERS

Stung by wire. Ordered back.
A Colonel's son from Galloway is blown away in the attack
on Syracuse. Height, name and rank
buzz and crack through crickets, hornets, bullets, flak . . . to
    Scotland, and the final cable
brought by a slip of a maid to the Colonel at the lochan.
    He confessed he drank
that night, the bulls broke out, the stags broke in,
    the beasts all bellowed brutal.

In the good old days, his rhodos shone
on Galdenoch! It's submerged in *ponticum* now, and
    the Colonel's family's gone –
unless you count old Jim, on his late mother's bike,
    peddling free-range eggs.
How she'd fash to see the state of it now, her thoroughbred
    machine an old boneshaker!
The Colonel was bound to send her away, when he'd grasped
    the bad news, and her legs.
This was the note he gave with the bike: 'God forgive the girl
    who tempted me to take her.'

Catherine Simpson

FEMALE: INSANE
From the journal of Dr William Hessle

15th June 1836

I have been honoured by an invitation to address the Edinburgh
Phrenological Society at its October meeting and must turn my thoughts
to a suitable subject.

Also today I received correspondence from a Mr Stephen Dalton,
governor of the Canongate Gaol, asking for help with the case of a
Frances MacNulty. MacNulty is currently incarcerated in his care,
awaiting trial for murder.

I replied immediately; agreeing to visit Mr Dalton at the gaol on
Tuesday. Having never before entered such an establishment, I am alive
with anticipation!

For dinner this evening, Mary served a most satisfactory mutton pie.
We had a lively game of cribbage.

19th June 1836

A fascinating day.

I arrived at Canongate Gaol two hours before noon as arranged. The
gaol is in poor repair; the walls exude dampness and a noxious odour
prevails. There are terrible shouts and the wails of the prisoners and
the clanking of their fetters are constant. It is the meanest place
and would have caused a lowering of my spirits had I not been there
on such a diverting excursion.

Dalton escorted me to a cell where I viewed Frances MacNulty
through a spyhole. MacNulty was seated upon a chair, gazing at a Bible
in her hands. She was wearing a cotton dress with a pinafore, a shawl
and work boots. Her hair was deep auburn in colour and tied neatly
at the nape of her neck.

Mr Dalton informed me of the details of the MacNulty case; apolo-
gising for the sordid nature of the events. He provided me with a report
from the *Scotsman* newspaper, which I affix here.

NEW TOWN MURDER
MAID SHOOTS GROOM IN JEALOUS FURY

Frances Margaret MacNulty was arrested at Heriot
Row, Edinburgh, last Wednesday evening for shooting
groom Jonathan Miller with a flintlock belonging to the
master of the house, Gerald McCrombie Esq. MacNulty,
aged 23, and Miller, 28, had apparently been involved in
a relationship of an improper nature for some time.
Witnesses claim that MacNulty had gone to the Green
Dragon public house to buy a flagon of ale for the house-
hold's evening meal. There she learned that Miller had
been seen with seamstress Helen Blythe. On becoming
suspicious that Miller was locked in the mews cottage
with Blythe, MacNulty banged repeatedly on the door
shouting words to the effect of: 'Come out, Johnny Miller.
I know what you're doing.' When Miller refused to open
the door, MacNulty stood on an upended bucket and
peered through the transom. Upon seeing Miller with
Blythe, MacNulty took the gun from her pinafore pocket
and fired three times through the door. Witnesses said
MacNulty then set up a weeping, which was most fearsome
to hear. Miller died later from gunshot wounds to the
abdomen. MacNulty was arrested at the scene and charged
with wilful murder. She was taken to the Canongate
Gaol to await trial, which is expected to take place in a
fortnight. If found guilty, MacNulty will face the ultimate
sanction of the law.

I was already aware of the case. However, I could not have imagined
the impact of seeing MacNulty for myself. I felt a jolt: of anxiety? Shock?
I know not; except that she cut a frail figure and it was impossible to
picture her drawing a weapon in anger.

Dalton seemed concerned for her welfare; segregating her for her
own good. MacNulty is from the lower orders but Dalton does not
believe she would survive in the main body of the gaol.

He had called me in on his own initiative after two other doctors refused to diagnose MacNulty as insane. Under the 'Criminal Lunatics Act' this would ensure incarceration at Her Majesty's Pleasure. Instead it appears that MacNulty will be tried as sane and no doubt found guilty, resulting in the inevitable penalty.

It seems Dalton has been inspired to 'save' MacNulty by a recent visit from Mrs Elizabeth Fry, who brought a number of Bibles to the gaol; including the one in MacNulty's hands.

Dalton is a staunch Christian and appears affected by Mrs Fry's entreaties for prison reforms and by MacNulty's refusal to let go of the Bible since it was placed in her hands. Apparently MacNulty will speak no words to Dalton except to talk of Jonathan Miller as though he were still alive.

Dalton asked if there was anything our science could do to prove that MacNulty had acted outwith her own will when she fired the gun.

I was, of course, delighted by this challenge and agreed to carry out phrenological examinations upon MacNulty forthwith.

Hence, I have arranged to revisit the prison tomorrow.

I am intrigued indeed! This promises to be a fascinating study and may offer a fine paper to be presented at the Edinburgh Phrenological Society come October.

This evening Mary produced a rich mutton stew served with a glass of Burgundy. Most satisfactory.

20th June 1836

I arrived at the gaol this morning before the old bell chimed nine o'clock.

MacNulty was sitting in her cell as yesterday, head bowed over her Bible. It was all I could do to persuade her to look straight ahead for the examination. She spoke not at all – not even in greeting.

My examination was systematic; I stood at MacNulty's right side, manipulating her head with my left hand and noting measurements with my right. I take pride in the sensitivity of my touch and liken my examinations to the playing of a musical instrument – a harp perhaps, or a pianoforte.

It took some time to get the necessary measurements; indeed I repeated the examination several times to ensure all was correct. MacNulty sat in silence throughout. Even when I asked if there was anything I could bring for her, or any other help I could offer, she spoke not at all.

At noon, having checked and rechecked the measurements, I left MacNulty to her Bible.

I asked Dalton if MacNulty's ancestors had shown signs of madness or were alcoholics. But he said MacNulty apparently arrived from Ireland some years ago and refused mention of any family.

This evening I went over my findings and can confirm what I suspected: MacNulty has an overdeveloped Organ of Combativeness and a weak intellect. This combination creates an unstable mind – in the manner of an argumentative child – and therefore I believe she would not be able to reason right from wrong. Consequently, I would argue she did not understand the true nature of her actions when she shot Miller.

Such a diagnosis, if accepted by the court, would give rise to the verdict: 'Not Guilty by Reason of Insanity'.

Mary served roast fowl for dinner, but I find I am without appetite.

21st June 1836

Having received free rein from Dalton, I revisited the gaol today to reconfirm my measurements. I again manipulated the organs of the brain with great delicacy.

MacNulty sat in silence even when I implored her: 'Frances, if you have any insanity running in your blood I beg you to make it known to the authorities for your own sake.' But she stared at the Bible open upon the table. The examination took a considerable time. I left her in the late afternoon.

I asked Mary not to produce a heavy dinner – merely a decanter of port. The girl has been clattering about the house in an infernal manner all evening. Is a man denied peace even in his own home?

22nd June 1836

I visited the gaol again today taking olive oil, combs, bowls, spoons, knives, extra-fine plaster of Paris and the box. If I am to use the MacNulty case for the Edinburgh Phrenological Society meeting, I will need a mould.

Despite appearing alarmed when I instructed her to let her hair loose and comb the oil through, Frances lay down her Bible and did as she was bid. Her hair is as soft as silk. When it was smooth I explained that I must lubricate her face with the oil and tallow. She closed her eyes and I ran the oil brush across her forehead, over her brows, down either side of her nose, across her lips and chin, across both cheeks and below her ears.

I mixed the plaster of Paris and explained the necessity of lying on the table with her neck resting in the mould box. She subjected herself to this and I poured in the plaster. I then inserted the goose quills up her nostrils, and the cotton in her ears, being as gentle as possible, so as not to alarm her, before brushing the plaster across her face. She lay still, not a muscle moving.

When the cast was removed, I hastened home to create the plaster head.

I have it before me now – flawless and smooth – a perfect head. Perfect. Frances Margaret MacNulty.

Mary is slacking – the port decanter was empty before ten o'clock.

23rd June 1836

I returned to the gaol. I implored Frances yet again to inform the authorities that she comes from an unstable family, to strengthen our case for a diagnosis of insanity.

She stared at her Bible, gently rocking back and forth, saying nothing. In frustration I shouted that Miller only got what he deserved, whereupon she looked me in the eye for the first time and stated: 'No! Johnny is a good man and I love him.'

I was astounded. For a second I could only stare at her. Then – as patiently as I could – I explained that 'Johnny' was in fact dead and whether she loved him or not was of no consequence. For a second she looked stricken and I almost felt badly for having spoken the truth. Then her face closed and she went back to the rocking and staring at her Bible.

I am afraid I continued to remonstrate with her; begging her to turn her thoughts from Miller and to consider herself. Also, to consider me and the efforts to which I was going on her behalf. She need not go to the gallows! I could save her, if only she would let me.

It was clear my entreaties went unheard and Frances would not deign to talk to me, so I left the gaol. I walked blindly for some considerable time, and I didn't find myself at home until nearly seven this evening.

I am now in my study looking at the head of Frances Margaret MacNulty. It has dried to a pure white; a perfect example. I have labelled it for the Society lecture, 'Female: Insane.'

24th June 1836

Returned to the gaol. Watched Frances through the spyhole. She stared blindly at that Bible of hers. I studied her without her knowledge for an hour or more. A guard had the audacity to ask me my business, to which I replied it was no damned concern of his.

25th June 1836

The trial draws near – only a week remains. I have yet to give my report to Dalton as I was hoping to furnish him with more information regarding the madness of the MacNulty family to back up my own findings of insanity.

I will visit the gaol again tomorrow. I must prevail upon Frances to talk to me. I must beg her. I must.

26th June 1836

Frances refuses to talk – but if she does it is to talk of that infernal Miller as though he were still alive! I have ordered her to desist. I have told her he is dead and that's an end to it, but she's obsessed. Obsessed!

Why does she persist? Miller is dead! Only I can save her, yet she throws my help back in my face with her silence and mention of that man. She must forget Miller!

I will return to the gaol tomorrow. I will make her see it is only me who can help her now.

I will make her forget Jonathan Miller.

I will wipe him away.

27th June 1836

It is difficult to write because of the bandage on my hand and the throbbing from the lacerations on my temple, but I must confess I was wrong about MacNulty; quite wrong.

Since returning from the gaol, I have reanalysed my measurements and indeed it seems MacNulty has an overdeveloped Organ of Destructiveness and is deficient in Conscientiousness. Her Organ of Amativeness is also overdeveloped and is combined with a weak morality.

These factors have allowed MacNulty to choose the life of a deceiver and a destroyer. She is a woman with a vicious tongue capable of making wild and wicked accusations – even against those much higher than herself in the social order. ~~She is a woman who doesn't~~ She is a woman capable of much physical violence even when unprovoked. Totally unprovoked.

MacNulty has chosen to embrace wickedness.

I have been working on my paper. It is entitled: 'The Interesting Case of the Wilful Murderess, Frances Margaret MacNulty'. I have made right the label, removing 'Female: Insane' and replacing it with 'Female: Extreme Cunning'.

Mary has replenished my decanter.

I must call her; I have been neglecting my dear Mary.

Morelle Smith

TIBOR ON THE TRAIN
Near the Hungarian border with Serbia

I knew from the high-visibility jacket that he threw onto the seat opposite me that he was some kind of official. That's why I'd asked him when I saw him get on, if the train was going to wait here for a while. I'd gone out into the corridor to speak to him. The somewhat serious expression on his face changed – his smile wrapped his eyes in a complicit almost mischievous grin, and he shrugged his shoulders. He did not speak English and I did not speak Hungarian. *Dober dan* I try, as we are after all not far from the Serbian border. He laughs and repeats this, and we *dobra dobra* to each other for a while. I try French then German, but he does not speak them either. *Italiano* he then says, *poco*. So we settle on Italian but it seems he knows even less than me, in fact the only phrase in Italian he seems to know is *bella ragazza*, which he says to me, nodding and smiling.

He then follows me back to my compartment, which I've had to myself up to then. He throws his luminous yellow jacket on the seat opposite, closes the compartment door and sits down two seats away, then moves into the one next to me. I want to distract his attention from me so I point to his jacket. He shows me what's written on the back in Hungarian, which means nothing to me. Train official? I say. *Labore in treni?* He laughs and says, pointing to himself, police, police. He then opens the small black pack that's attached to his belt, and pulls out a gun and handcuffs, laughing all the time. Oh wonderful! I laugh with him, though he may not have picked up on my irony, as the thought of being alone in a compartment with an overfriendly policeman with handcuffs does not rate highly on my list of favourite situations.

But he has a distraction, and this turns out to be an elderly couple in the next compartment. He opens the door and beckons to me. An old man is walking away from us, along the corridor. Problem, he says – border – and he gestures to show that he will be put off at the border. But he's old! I protest. He shakes his head and repeats the cutting-off gesture. Papers, he says, papers – no. At Kelebia, the border with Serbia, he will escort them off, so I gather from his gestures.

But that's still a few kilometres away. He sits down next to me again. Tibor, he says, pointing to himself. And you? – he points to me. I tell him my name. Phone? he says. He writes down his phone number on a piece of paper, and gestures to me to write down mine, which I do. The thought crosses my mind that I could write down the wrong number but I decide it won't do any harm to put the correct one. Then I'm glad I did, for he immediately pulls out his phone and dials my number. It rings and he is delighted with this. He gestures to me to phone his number, and it's fun and games as we play with our phones. More fun as the train jerks a little and he exaggerates the rocking movement and falls against me. *Bella ragazza* he repeats, leans closer and tries to kiss me. I hold up my hand and try to look suitably stern. He leans back and salutes. Then takes my hand and kisses it. He pulls out his phone again and shows me the photograph on it. It's of him, and his German shepherd dog. I nod enthusiastically. *Cane* I say, pointing to the dog. *Cane?* he asks. I nod. He then roars with laughter and points to himself. *Cane* – me, he says.

The train has slowed down, and he realises that we're at Kelebia, the border, and he grabs his high-visibility jacket and he's off. A few seconds later he's back, remembering the couple next door. I hear him talking to them. He passes in the corridor again, throws a kiss and a *ciao* into the compartment. Outside, more waves and thrown kisses from the platform.

The elderly couple get off and place their bags on the ground. The man heads towards the building. Border police get on and check people's passports. About fifteen minutes later, the old man walks back along the platform, waving a piece of paper. He talks to some other policemen standing outside, and then to my relief he, his wife and their bags get back on the train. Tibor waves and throws a last kiss, as the train moves slowly out of the station.

Sarah Smith

SON OF THE MARS

The sounds of The Mars linger in his head. They lurk in an unfathom-
able space in his brain, surfacing only occasionally: a clatter of heavy
cutlery on the bottom of a porcelain sink; the early-morning shriek of
hungry gulls; the whisper of an iron plane as it glides through wood.
They bubble up through grey water – these everyday noises – endlessly
repeating on a loop. Over the years, he has packed his head full of other
places and different people, attempting to erect a soundproof barrier
against the insistent blether from The Mars.

*

The *Mars* training ship looks ancient. Otherworldly, like something
out of an adventure story. Nine-year-old Charlie McBride sits in an
open cart by the shore on the Fife bank of the River Tay. To the north,
the outlined city of Dundee lies so far in the distance that he finds it
incomprehensible that it is the same place they came from this morning.
The underside of his thighs rub bare against a splintered wooden seat
and the skin around his knees is damp and mottled with cold. He stares
at the black and white ship, imagining huge cannons fired on the barked
orders of uniformed officers and scurvy-ridden, press-ganged men
scrabbling up rigging to adjust the sails and keep the old hulk on course.
In the forenoon of Thursday the 18th of February 1909, Charlie attempts
to refashion his punishment as an exciting voyage on the high seas.

   Mr Simons, who has travelled in the cart with Charlie and three
other boys from Dundee, gets down from his seat and pays the driver.
He gestures to the boys to follow him. Charlie grabs his meagre belongings, wrapped tightly in a piece of sacking and tied with a length of
dark green webbing, and follows Mr Simons towards the water. They
tramp along a pier as, behind them, cartwheels and horses' hooves
combine to make an inelegant turn, scramble through shingle, and
finally clatter back onto the narrow main road. Mr Simons untethers
a large rowing boat and climbs down, steadying himself and the craft
by holding on to a ragged post sticking out of the water.

'In you get, lads. One at a time.'

Mr Simons reaches up and helps the boys down into the boat, indicating where they should sit to get the balance right. Lastly, he sits down himself, lays his jacket over his lap, plants his feet hip-width apart and slides the oars into position.

'Push us off, son,' he says, nodding at a heavy-set boy at the back of the boat. 'Give it a right good shove.'

It takes twenty minutes or so to row out to the ship. The *Mars* is anchored off Woodhaven Harbour near Wormit. All four boys silently watch Mr Simons' forearms pulse back and forth as he works the oars. Charlie sits directly in front of Mr Simons, alongside a boy of about the same age as himself, while the two other, bigger boys sit on the narrower seats at either end of the boat. The muscles in Mr Simons' wiry arms move as efficiently as pistons. The oars cut like blades through butter but heavy beads of sweat at Mr Simons' temples betray the true extent of his effort. Meanwhile, the stationary boys shiver, as the air around them grows colder and colder.

As they near the ship, the dark wood of the hull seems to envelop them, blocking out the faraway city on the far shore until they are sandwiched between its blistered surface and the wide expanse of glassy water they have just crossed.

Mr Simons rows slower, steering the boat alongside a rope ladder. He looks at Charlie.

'You need to climb up to the top, son. Stand up now.'

He takes Charlie's bundle, unwraps it, and finds a worn, leather belt that once belonged to Charlie's father. Mr Simons repackages the belongings and makes a rudimentary backpack by tying the bundle to the belt and strapping it across Charlie's body.

'Dinna worry, McBride. Take your time and you'll be all right.'

Charlie stands in the boat, his legs threatening to buckle, and finds himself utterly unable to take a step forward. Mr Simons takes his hand and places it on the side of the ladder. The rope is huge, so thick that Charlie's fingers cannot stretch to meet its width, but he holds on and begins to move.

'Keep moving. One step at a time.'

Mr Simons stands behind him and cups Charlie's shoulder.

'See, the best way to do it, son,' he says quietly, 'is to look straight in front of you and think about the supper you'll get the night.'

At first, Charlie counts the steps but, as he gets higher, the ladder slips and sways beneath him and he finds it difficult to remember which number comes next. He hears his mother's voice counting, teaching him numbers as she feeds the baby in their room at Quarry Pend, off the Cowgate. Charlie is four and his sister Nellie not long born, always crying for food or warmth or company. Her tiny hand forms a vice-like grip around Charlie's offered finger and now he dredges up a similar strength, holding on to the damp, greasy rope, inching painfully upwards, until he finally reaches the top, where strange hands scoop him on to the deck. Bearded faces scrutinise him for a few moments until he is pushed roughly to the side while they turn back to the ladder and their next recruit.

Once they are all aboard, Captain Lawson delivers a cursory introduction and the new boys are taken below. A disorientated Charlie emerges an hour or so later, with a haircut and thoroughly scrubbed person, clothed in the ship's uniform of tunic, long trousers and necktie. Extra clothes and other equipment are issued to him and stowed in a sack. Everything, including the hammock that will be his bed, is marked with a number. Two hundred and seventy-two. From the moment of admission, he ceases to be called by his own name and is always addressed by this number, even by his shipmates. They drop the hundred and contract syllables, until even boys who come from as far afield as Glasgow and Inverness pronounce the numbers in a heavy Dundonian accent. Twa-sna-twa is on this ship. Charlie McBride is not on this ship. He is given into the care of a group of initiated boys, who take him to the dining room, where tea, milk and biscuits fill his stomach but do not calm his nerves.

In spite of the strange sensation of lying in a hammock, he sleeps all the way through the first night, but tears sting his face on waking. In the admissions ledger it is written that he is nine years of age, deserted by his father, has a mother who works at a mill and has an infant to support; he has been ill-fed, is in rags, can neither read nor write, and is likely to become involved in petty crime. His previous character is described as uncontrolled and neglected. His height is four foot seven inches and his figure is stout with fair complexion, brown hair and hazel eyes. He wipes his face and tries not to think of his mother pushing cloths into gaping windows to stop the draughts.

Charlie soon learns that each Mars day is much like the next. Only the weather changes.

*

Friday, 6th June 1912 and the boys leave the ship for their annual holiday at Elie. Charlie has been to Elie three times before and is looking forward to it. Seven days with no work, no lessons and no shipboard rations. He prays for good weather so that he can run across the pure expanse of Elie beach and plunge his bare feet deep into the grains of the earth. If he is lucky and the sun shines, everything will be tinder-dry: the red brick of the granary store gifted to them by a benevolent local businessman; the striped bedding in their makeshift dormitories; the soles of their boots as they walk smartly to church on Sunday; the blushed stone of the harbour wall as it bakes their skin.

Three hundred uniformed boys are ferried from the *Mars* and then march over twenty miles north to south through the burgh of Fife. They leave Woodhaven in the morning, and tramp via Guardbridge, Peat Inn, and Largoward, halting at an interval of rest at each of these places.

At Elie, he watches holidaymakers on the beach. Courting couples, groups of elderly ladies and gentlemen and families from the linoleum factories in Kirkcaldy and coalmining towns that pepper the landscape for miles around. These city dwellers arrive like refugees, desperate to jump into clean water, but the *Mars* boys cleave to the land like an alien race, relishing their freedom to roam. Like spiders who have been carelessly swept down a plughole and have negotiated the precarious footholds leading back to the surface, the boys are determined to put as much distance between themselves and the sea as possible. Instead, they play all day and into the evening on the beach. Games are organised by the officers: sprinting, leap-frog, rounders, football. Football is the best as far as Charlie is concerned. He sometimes plays in his dreams, so much does he miss it aboard ship.

He remembers playing with other lads in Quarry Pend on days when he was sent out from under his mother's feet and, later, on waste-ground behind factories when he should have been at the school. A makeshift ball thudding on cobbles, ricocheting off walls and trapped in a tangle of limbs and swear words. Knackered afterwards, they wandered through streets, scavenged at pubs for cigarette douts and came up with elaborate ideas as they sucked on the taste of smoke and residue of cheap alcohol. Feeling grown-up they pilfered some lengths of rope from a cart in the High Street and sold them down the docks, jumped a queer fellow for the money in his wallet in an alley just off the Cowgate and graduated to thieving from shops and the open windows of villas on the outskirts of the city.

The football match at Elie is glorious. The boys are organised into two full teams and sweep across the sand, dribbling and passing. Using their *Mars* numbers to communicate, they attract curious glances from a crowd of spectators.

'Ower here, twa-erry-seeven,' shouts Charlie.

The ball glances off his foot and crosses the goal line.

'Twa-sna-twa. Ye wee beauty!'

For a few seconds, Charlie is ambushed by his teammates but they quickly spread out again, eager for the game to keep moving. He flexes his toes, gripping a strand of dry, knobbly seaweed so that it trails behind him as he returns to the melee. On board ship the hold often serves as a gymnasium and Charlie likes the drills and the chance to perform on the bars and the horse, but playing football on the beach at Elie is a lantern-slide entertainment come to life.

*

He was Jonah in the belly of the whale. Patiently sitting it out. Waiting for deliverance and repenting for all he was worth. Keeping his nose clean, his head bowed, and singing every hymn they told him to. God had had the decency to spew out Jonah after three days and three nights. The Dundee authorities lacked the Big Man's work ethic and took their time. Charlie was released from The Mars almost five years later, two days after his fourteenth birthday.

*

Quarry Pend pales in January sunlight and Charlie finds his mother and sister gone. The wife on the ground floor tells him they left months since. Regardless, Charlie climbs the steps to the old room and pushes open the door. Inside he stands and stretches his arms up to the ceiling and then out to the sides, marvelling at how small the space has become. A piece of faded cloth that his mother stuffed into a gap at the window has worked loose and is balled up on the bed-frame. Charlie pulls it taut, releasing a cloud of acrid dust that fizzes in a shaft of light cutting through the gloom. He lays the cloth back down on the springs and stares at the pattern the elements have painted on it, tracing the protected lines of colour that remain, a secret map back to that which he has lost.

He leans against a damp, stone wall and takes papers from his inside pocket. A letter of introduction to a Mr Paterson, supervisor at the cooperage where an apprenticeship has been arranged for him, and a similar letter addressed to a Mrs Coutts, who has a room for Charlie to board in. He folds both letters up again and returns them to the safety of his jacket. From behind his ear, he retrieves the farewell cigarette gifted to him by the harbour master at Woodhaven and lights it with a match from a box by the stove. He smokes in silence until he has no choice but to admit it is time to go.

James P. Spence

THE DIRECTORY ON LEOPOLD PLACE

Because the deliverer couldn't get into the stair
it was left in its plastic by the door

Because no one entering thought to lift it
the directory leaned against the wall for months

Because it leaned against the wall for months
the wrapper grew as black as gutter slush

Because of the bus stop on the pavement
somebody waiting tore the wrapper off

Because it became litter a reveller
threw it on the shelter roof

Because at street level no one sees it
the directory has weathered there for months

Because the snows didn't come this winter
it hasn't bloated, buckled or blown away

Because my son insists on upstairs on the bus
I see the weather working through names A–Z

Sheila Templeton

WORKIN MEN

I miss thaim. Miss their quait
haans restin lowssed
oan dusty overalls
deen wi the day's wark,
wachty buits ackwart
in their sklaik o glaur
or pentit spleiter;
the carefu wye they sat
on buses, gaan hame.

My granda's waak
the pleesure o his waak
his hertsome dander up Station Road
lang widden jyner's rule pokin oot
the nairra pooch o his dungers
spleet-new saadist furrin his jaicket.

An my faither, tall chiel
swingin alang a hyne-awa railway line
lang sicht taakin swatch o aathing
unner his ontak; fish-plates, bowts,
ivery sleeper in its cinner bed,
on the keevee for onything amissin
– yet his een shairp-set
oan the blae far-awa, the mischancie
o twa bairns, heelster-gowdie
ower steel-glaizie rails –
now racin lik a pair o slung-stanes
tae walcome his hame-comin.

WAR RECORD

Mairzy doats and dozy doats and liddle lamzy divey
A kiddley divey too, wooden shoe?

They say that American servicemen used its lyrics as passwords.
But we used it for dancing and showing our knickers
me and Great-Auntie Lizzie – hers shell-pink celanese
elasticated at the knee, astonished at being on parade.

Words. Ciphers. Codes. Stuttering like guns; wheeling like birds.

Sic a pastin Aiberdeen Harbour took the nicht afore you were born.
I listened the hale o that nicht tae it. The soond o their engines.
Heinkels. The grun shaakin.

Even now, a small place deep inside, tissue memory
flinches hearing the weight of a slow droning plane.

Mammy and me scared witless in the juddering dark,
thin red tracer lines bisecting our garden sky, shivering
in Mrs Burnett's glass porch knocking and knocking.
Sherry for pregnant Mammy, cocoa for me.
Digestive biscuits. Sugar sprinkled thick
on buttered white plain loaf. Damp musty earth smell
and cold feet in the Anderson shelter.

Ach the Hun'll nivver bomb us.
We've the mock aerodrome up at the Moss.
They've been drappin aathing they've got up there!

My beautiful square-shouldered aunties scarlet-lipped,
fake stocking-ed American Tan
and seams drawn on with eyebrow pencil.
Quiet Grunnie telling Mr Jenkins the Minister
in plain public view *she widnae be back tae his Kirk*
if he couldna manage een one refugee in that reamin great manse...

Granda in his ARP tin helmet. Daddy watching for fires
all along the railway line. Reserved occupations.
Powdered egg. Gas masks in boxes. A dance frock
sewn in secret from parachute silk.
Mum's the word for stealthy yellow farm butter.

Passwords. Codes. Ciphers. Mysteries.

Tia Thomson

GIFT

Finding that tiny flower
on this steep hillside –
above, snow-topped mountains,
Loch Tay so still below;

Softly busy birdsong
sheep grazing,
a tinkling lower down:
Sun warms my shoulders
this Mother's Day, far from home.

My father loved the hills
– he'd have seen this view on
a Perthshire-coloured morning
with this deer, and echoes
of Mac Mhaighstir Alasdair
and Donnchadh Bàn . . .

Stout walking shoes
knew every inch and hollow,
he'd watch the deer run,
how they'd stop –
and listen:

She edges closer, knows
I'm here, unhurried:
a lone curlew passes.

Tia Thomson

TÌODHLAC

Thachairt ri flùr beag bìodach ud
air an t-slighe chas seo –
os mo chionn, beinn bhàrr-gheal,
cho balbh, Loch Tàtha fodham:

Eun-ciùil socair trang,
caoraich a' feurachadh
gliongartaich nas ìsle:
blàths na grèine air mo ghualainn
Làtha na Màthair 's mi air seachran.

Laigh gràdh m' athair air a' bheinn
– chitheadh esan an sealladh seo
air madainn Shiorrachd-Pheairteach
leis am fiadh seo, is mac-talla
Mhic Mhaighstir Alasdair
is Dhonnchaidh Bhàin . . .

Brògan làidir na coiseachd
eòlach air gach lag is òirleach,
bhiodh a' coimhead air
ruith na fèidh, 's iad a' sgur
's ag èisteachd:

Ceum air cheum na b' fhaisge,
àireach orm, mì-ghreasach:
chaidh guilbneach seachad na aonar.

Aisha Tufail

BUCKET BATH

I lift my son into the bath and watch him sit on a small plastic stool.

'Bucket bath today, *Amma*?'

'Yes *sonay*, bucket bath today.'

Inside my long English bath sits a plastic ten-litre tub. I fill up the tub, first with hot, then cold water until it is warm water. Then I lather up the soap by spinning it in my hands and proceed to spread soft, white bubbles over him. The way my mum used to.

We used to live in a flat in the city centre of Glasgow. It was an office floor which my father had rather ingeniously converted into a home for us. I remember an old cupboard that had been tiled and made into a walk-in shower. On the wall hung a showerhead and on the floor sat a plastic bucket with a plastic jug in it, bobbing on the water. Two small wooden stools sat beside this bathing paraphernalia.

We children would come, one at a time, and sit on one wooden stool. My mother would be sitting on the other stool and now I can see her again, she is spinning a thin piece of soap in her hand to work up a lather. With one hand she holds me as if I were about to escape and with her other hand she works the lather into my skin. It feels as if it is being forced into my bones. She doesn't believe in sponges but rather prefers to massage the muck out of us. Her hands are big and strong, not cruel, but just impatient, with other, more important things to do. Now she is filling the jug with water with one hand and pouring water over me, rinsing me clean. I clench my eyes shut, for fear of soap getting into them.

But I think deeper now and place my mother on a wooden stool in Pakistan in my grandparents' home. It is a double-storey building now, but I can remember it when it was a single-storey building, with rooms built at one end and the *ghuslkhana* and *latrine*, two separate rooms, at the other end. I have been to this home many times but the images I conjure up now are from my own personal memory and stories passed down. My mother is an older sister to three brothers. She is young at this time, I know, but I can't help making her look as she is today.

I imagine my maternal uncle sitting in the *ghuslkhana* on a stool, being bathed by her. I use the image of the young, brown body of my brother and steal my uncle's face from a photograph I have saved in my mind to create a picture of him. She proceeds to lather him, using a pink bar of Lifebuoy soap. It has the smell of the pink carbolic soap from my primary school toilets. The water bucket is steel and is filled with cold tap water. The steel jug bobs on the water.

I can see as she washes him. Young and beautiful and strong. Soon to leave for unseen lands far away. To live with a man she doesn't know but is married to. To watch snow fall from the sky for the first time. To shed soft tears at night from the pain of separation, from her family, her home, her everything. To stand at market stalls selling Shetland jumpers with my father. I look into a cardboard box and see myself. She says I would just sit for the whole time in that box, behind the market stall. Again I see her, lifting bread-baskets in the morning into a newsagent's. Making long-distance phone calls to hear the voices of her mother and father drowned in crackles in the line.

'Done, *Amma*?'

'Yes, we're done.'

I watch as the water pours slowly down the drain. Gone for ever.

I wrap my cleansed son in a warm towel, lift him out and hold him close to me. The softness of the towel touches me and for a moment I feel it around me as well.

Amma – Mother (Urdu)
sonay – dear (Urdu)
ghuslkhana – bathroom (Urdu)
latrine – toilet room (Urdu)

David Underdown

BOTHY LANDS

Peanmeanach, Leacraithnaich,
Strathchailleach, Staoineag, Craig . . .

Across the firth the Quiraing's jigsaw fret
is topped again by April snows
just as when families arrived
to claim their Homes for Heroes.

All over now: moors marching back
from scoured shingle, lousewort and broomrape
clinging on. For fear of falling masonry
the house is closed with health and safety tape.

Out in the Minch the famished gannets gorge on plastic
line their guts with shreds of carrier bags.
Inland, stacked beach-high behind the tide lines,
cartons, a lube oil drum among the yellow flags.

The bridge has gone – a lone Lands Ender
heading south was almost drowned –
but though the talk's of open access
all futures now are settled on the Mound –

glens bright with plans,
bankers talking dirty down in Edinburgh
of how they'll bring the salmon
back to how they were.

Birders scan the empty shorelines
toting top Swarovski bins.
Sharks sieve thinning seas for plankton,
thresh accusatory fins.

Peanmeanach, Leacraithnaich,
Strathchailleach, Staoineag, Craig . . .

Ryan Vance

FINCH AND CROW DO THE ALLEYCAT

Tiptoe on tarmac, other foot pulling pedals to starting position, Crow hunches over drop bars, waits in downpour and dark for the lights to change.

'You're doing it wrong!' shouts Remmy from behind.

Crow can't see the other cyclist coming at him, stripped of all reflectors, dayglo clothing, but he's there, balanced on Great Western's dashed centre line. Suck of air, spray of roadwater. Remmy dives past, headlong into traffic, takes the lead in the Glasgow Alleycat.

He's not about to take advice from Remmy of all people, on this night of all nights. Red, amber, green. He pushes off.

Several more racers zip past, no momentum sacrificed to the Kelvinbridge crossing. Crow's watch beeps. He should've passed first checkpoint by now. If he wants to shadow Finch, he'll have to speed up.

Held on Hallowe'en and Valentine's, the Alleycat's as close to tradition as the messenger community veers. The job attracts impatient people, transient souls, thrill-seekers, urban warriors, political radicals, shady folk who prefer cash in hand, no licence plates. That twice a year they can be corralled to the starting line in Kelvingrove Park is nothing short of a miracle; not such a surprise most assembled then choke back a cocktail of pills and booze before push-off.

Not Crow; a long nap and a double-shot espresso was enough. Some laughed at the starting line when he declined a communal swig of Buckie, but most held their tongue. They probably think they know why tonight is important to Crow, but they've no idea.

Because while this is Crow's first Alleycat, strictly speaking he's not even racing.

He's retracing. Following Finch, riding his long-faded tyretracks. Sort of.

Fastest courier in Glasgow, Finch had bragged. He'd earned the title by way of charmed negligence, ignoring red lights, hopping kerbs. He'd been a menace to the public in broad daylight, never mind a suicidal showboating of two-wheeled gallusness. Not that his eight-year run of Alleycat triumphs was any sort of proof. Plotting the route from behind a locked door definitely gave him an edge, and Crow'd discovered Finch outright cheated when it came to collecting the full deck.

But check out his client list: city-wide, high profile, twice the pick-ups of any other courier in the city. His shoulder-holstered walkie-talkie never stopped buzzing. Go here. Go there. Go everywhere. Just don't give him anything particularly fragile, not unless you wanted it delivered with enough scrapes and scars to match his face.

The weeks after his disappearance it must have seemed the city was stuck in mud.

That's the sort of loon Crow's chasing, this dank October night. Chasing, or replacing, he isn't certain.

Every working day he wondered if through some unseen connection he might sense the exact moment a speeding windscreen or unchecked wing mirror cracked open Finch's skull. No point protesting, telling him to be careful. It was as if Finch himself had no say in the matter.

Now Crow only knows he must follow, to rejoin the man he lost to uncalculated risk.

By the time they'd met, Finch had earned his nickname, and it wasn't difficult to see how the crew settled on Crow for the new recruit. Crow played the straight man to Finch's hairpin curves. You'd ask Finch to deliver a heart on ice, Crow to carry the ash-filled urn. The unlikeliness of the pairing was its own inevitable sort of story, a downhill freewheeling.

And then, last Hallowe'en, Finch . . . flew away.

Crow still doubts what he saw last Hallowe'en. Standing at the finish line at the foot of Hope Street, he'd peeked out from under the Hielanman's majestic steel and glass Umbrella. The clouds were low, the rain was heavy. In the middle of the street, back and shoulders steaming sweat, his thighs pumping, there was Finch.

And then, a glimmer later, he wasn't.

It took six months of days that felt like slipped gears for Crow to accept Finch wasn't coming back.

They hadn't raced on Valentine's for obvious reasons, but Finch's route didn't work in February anyway. It had to be Hallowe'en. That's what Crow's spent this last year figuring out, what he's putting to the test tonight.

He curves past the Botanic Gardens onto Byres Road. Ditched bikes cluster the corner, their Alleycat owners fighting over a ziplock sandwich bag tied to one of the park's fences. Inside the ziplock there's two dozen cards showing a fool in rags, clutching a rod, walking blind over a cliff. Crow had thought it clever how Finch always used the Rider tarot deck to mark checkpoints; turns out that's the only deck that works. The other twenty-one major arcana are strung up around the city, awaiting pick-up. A full deck for every racer.

Well – almost. Finch did love a shortcut.

Crow feels an ache apart from the ghost of fatigue.

He coasts past the park. The Alleycatters shout after him, Remmy's voice above all others: 'That's not the way!'

The way? What does he know? Remmy, the most-kinked chain in the gang, who in seeking protection from other road users earned his nickname by hugging the sides of buses like remora to a shark, who'd once headbutted a policewoman in the Royal Wedding riots? Fuck Remmy.

He has no idea, no idea at all, what designs their wheels now draw across the skin of the city. What the route unlocks. Finch knew. Now Crow knows. But how close has he to follow Finch?

Another red light looms at Hillhead subway; halts him. The Underground belches students in costume. Crow remembers Hallowe'en parties, a checkpoint in itself, one of many arranged in a never-ending loop. Just get to Christmas. Just get to Easter. Expect something to change. Hope against reason for some city council to build you an overpass out of routine. Don't look where you're going.

Crow wills the light to change, seconds slipping into the night.

It wasn't for the rush that Crow became a messenger. He wanted the other side of the street: to feel like he owned the city, or that it owned him.

So many other people took the same routes to the same jobs, homes, pubs and gyms for years, never really connecting with their environment, immediate, intermediate. Folded like origami, the entire city they knew could fit into one high-rise. Crow had lived that way: passed every exam, bagged every promotion, pinned pictures of friends to his cubicle wall, bought a one-bedroom flat and then – felt unmoored.

There was an expectation that if he followed the signposts to the good life, if he built that nest, the sunny bird of happiness would swoop down to occupy it. But the clouds stayed low, and the rain still fell. He'd been called to an uplift with no destination. At its heart, Glasgow approached permanence like a deliberate hit-and-run.

And then, a diversion.

Their receptionist quit one day. Didn't bother to show up. Crow was assigned to the front desk. In walked Finch: lycra-sleek, sweat-fresh. A transaction, a signature, a wink, and back out into the rain. Just like that. Unmoored in a completely different sense of the word.

Crow bought a bike. Crow bought a helmet. Crow bought lights and lycra and a bell. Crow signed up to a courier company, got his own walkie-talkie, gave himself over to the suck and push of transit, supply, demand. His body became functional. His sleep became smooth and dark as the freshest tarmac.

His understanding of Glasgow sprawled, from rattling, ratty service bays, with their rough humour, to pristine corporate high-rises, greeted by suits and pencil skirts, friendly but clipped as if sensing his rejection. The in-betweens, the dead spaces, the doors marked for staff only, for restricted access, for the loading of goods, almost all unlocked and opened. In kinship with the city he was second only to the binmen.

Life unfolded for Crow like a road map, and somewhere in the creases he'd found Finch, all thighs and knotted shoulders, a mind and heart like a fully stocked toolkit. They met for the second time in a pub. Finch gave Crow the once-over, said: 'Took you long enough.' Crow didn't feel the impact of affection until the shock wore off, but by then it was too late. Something had snapped and mended in the time it took Crow to flip a taxi the bird.

All this was not to say Finch was . . . undamaged.

'You know it's the craziest thing,' Crow said once, 'to have a room in your house you never let anyone inside?'

'Not the craziest, trust me,' Finch replied. 'That's on the other side.'

Twice a year Finch locked himself away to plot the Alleycat, new routes posted to a password-protected messageboard. In other cities Alleycats changed drastically each year but under Finch's direction, checkpoint changes were minimal, differences no more than a street or two.

'Why so cautious?' Crow asked.

'Fine-tuning,' said Finch.

Crow never thought to ask if Finch was fine-tuning something other than the Alleycat.

Then he'd disappeared into a crease of the map.

That's what it looked like: as if some unseen hand had scrumpled him up.

All it took to break into Finch's flat that night was one solid kick to the door – and after three years of daily cycling, boy, could Crow kick.

Looking back, Crow wonders if the police bothered trying to understand what they found in that room. It *was* crazy on the other side.

Hundreds of maps of Glasgow. Stuck to the walls, piled high on desks. Road maps. Aerial surveys. Hand-drawn. Google Maps printouts stapled together, covering an entire wall. All dissected by red Sharpie, some cut up and restuck, organised by year, or by time, whatever was necessary to make sense of the collage at any given moment.

Crow touched nothing, took pictures on his phone. He wasn't stupid.

Going through the images, it seemed nothing more innocent than an obsession with planning the race. That is, at any rate, what the cops would see: a reckless contest for adrenaline junkies. Maybe they dusted for prints then threw it all in the recycling, a lunatic's hobby.

But there were anomalies. One map was different from the others: the whole of Scotland, criss-crossed with ruler-straight markings, converging and splitting, like some twisted, sprung-spoked wheel. Knowing Finch's mystic streak, it wasn't difficult to guess these were leylines, divvying up the country along channels of ancient, unknown power.

Other documents, the older road maps, yellow and torn, had square chunks cut out of them. The absences were, well . . . absent. In a year of searching Crow never found these scraps. They must have been with

Finch when he vanished. To find the missing pieces, Crow tracked down duplicates of the maps online and in junk stores. Some were expensive collector editions but most were worthless, mapping a city now torn down and rebuilt, rerouted, inherently transient.

Collected and collated, the missing squares charted something stranger still.

A city that never had existed.

It was a trick to calm the paranoid mapmaker: fake roads and dummy landmarks included to identify copycats too diligent in their forgeries. Inner-city Glasgow's grid system somewhat limited this technique, but still the mapmakers found room for odd alleys and dead-ends.

For eight years Finch had led them on a hunt for these missing roads. The little shifts in Alleycat markers, a delicate circling in, spiralling in, closing in on all these null spaces. These streets led to nothing, and began there too. They'd been racing to nowhere.

But here's the thing about the Alleycat: it's a test of how well you know the streets – or, more often, the alternatives. There's proof of progress, but how you move between checkpoints is your own business. Pedestrianised zones, back alleys, launching yourself the wrong way down a one-way street, of which Glasgow was lousy – anything to get to that next baggie of tarot cards.

Knowing this, and knowing its architect, Crow spied something police could never have discovered, no matter how long they stared at these maps:

Twice a year, and twice a year only, on Valentine's and Hallowe'en, Finch took the scenic route.

There were some constants. Always crossing Glasgow Bridge, even if the Squinty Bridge further down the Clyde shaved at least three minutes off the route. Always once around George Square when he could just cut through it, dodging the hand-in-hand lovebirds or fall-over-drunk skeletons, depending on the season. Always uphill past the Necropolis where the leylines converged, its sentinel crypts presiding over the city. Always finish close to Central Station, often in the cobbled alley next to the Diamond Dolls strip joint. That last constant had been a mystery to Crow and the women in the group, but the lads never complained.

Now Crow understood. It wasn't the destinations that had mattered to Finch. It wasn't even the journey. It was some arcane meeting point between the two: completion.

The downhill slalom on Renfrew Street, always against the flow of traffic, was the last daredevil flourish in some citywide incantation, but there was no indication, none at all, that Finch ever knew what he was invoking.

Whatever it was, whatever door he had unlocked, it had slammed shut behind him.

And Crow had missed him so, so much.

So now he's following, forging ahead, as predictable and blind as when he first fell for that scar-faced trailblazer.

Coals alight in his thighs and back and shoulders, knuckles white and numb in the October rain. Lights glimmer, reflected under rubber, blurring red and green in the corners of his eyes. He doesn't stop to collect the tarot deck. Few of them are easy grabs: back of the Armadillo, up a fire escape on Lynedoch Street, an arm thrust through the fence at Trongate tower to scrabble for the ziplock spinning in the wet wind. If he stopped to collect each card he'd never make the final checkpoint in time, never mind the front of the pack. How had Finch done it? There was trickery afoot, that much was obvious, but the cheat was so blatant Crow had almost missed it.

This might be the scenic route but speed is still essential, small red time-trials scribbled on the maps. Some seem overly generous, most are borderline impossible, but three quarters to the finish, here comes Finch's breakthrough: a piece of city planning so disastrously stupid it's difficult to believe anyone ever deemed it fit for purpose.

A minute's zig-zagging south from Finnieston, all roads begin sloping south-east. Once upon a time they pointed to Central Station, a smooth blending of the lower city centre and affluent west. But back in the late sixties they pulled up half the city at the behest of big transit, and now these streets butt up perpendicular against the concrete cleft of the M8. A facepalm of logistics, cutting Argyle Street in half and mutating George's Cross in the process.

Chunks of unfinished off-ramps stick into the air like shattered bones poking through the city's skin. A short-sighted nightmare with no end. How many homes, marvels Crow as he approaches, how many lives must have been displaced for this cold and snaking hubris? How many constant, unexamined routes must have warped and twisted in the aftermath?

Too late, the council sought to suture with a ridiculous stitch of cycle path. Of course, it was too common sense to follow the natural roll of the land and reconnect the frayed ends of Argyle Street. No, no – this solution is more like a spine twisted in seizure. The green-floored strip-lit cage takes off in a dizzying spiral just before Anderston Station and bucks north over the M8, miles of traffic clotting underneath. The Waterloo Street exit doubles as an on-ramp for the motorway, flood-lights spurring traffic to speed into eight lanes of road rage, and fuck any oncoming obstacles.

That Glasgow City Council might try and actively exterminate cyclists with such a suicidal trick seemed unbelievable. Unless . . .

Was it more than simple traffic control?

Moving from the Anderston Alleycat checkpoint up to Blythswood Square meant counterintuitive backtracking, traffic jams, uphill wandering. However poorly implemented, this dumb cycle path was a resuscitation of older, faster passage through Finch's open-air labyrinth. In Finch's disappearing act, it was a sleight-of-hand.

Could there be others perfecting the same trick? Moving through City Halls' gold and marble chambers, rolls of Prussian blue paper tucked under their arms, swiping proposals on glassy tablets. Was someone else pitching and planning escape from the modern world?

Finch didn't care. All that mattered was the shortcut would get him where he needed to be.

If it didn't kill him.

Accelerating down the cycle path Crow stands on the pedals in a half-crouch. It spits him out onto an afterthought of pavement clustered with bollards and streetlights. He feints once, twice. No gaps in traffic. Tugs on brakes, hops off before the bus stop. One terrifying swerve through misted headlights—

Crow's watch beeps at him.

Must. Go. Faster.

He looks himself once over, from the inside. Something full of bullet points and definitions slips sideways off the saddle.

Took you long enough.

On the long straights he peels off from the double yellows and takes his place centre-street. White dashes hiss morse. It's a sly lean to the left, to the right, to dodge the bass-thumping plastic race-cars, the greasy white vans, the murderous taxis, the glacial buses. Fewer potholes. No pedestrians.

It's a truncated version of the city, but what a lumbering beast it was. Owning and being owned, moving as it moved, halting when it slowed – no. Better to live within it but not of it, to skim alongside, to bounce off its cracked and painted hide.

Uphill to the centre, Crow catches sight of Remmy on a parallel street. They match each other over the hump of Douglas Street down to Sauchiehall. Crow rejoins the race.

And it means nothing to him.

The Hallowe'en crowd stumbles into traffic, a jumble of foam-padded superheroes, devils in miniskirts. Remmy's ahead, barking insults at the jaywalkers. Who could blame him? Sauchiehall pedestrianises. Remmy peels off down Blythswood Street. Crow flies straight on. The crowd closes in. Car horns downshift to insults, thrust like sticks in his spokes.

Crow wefts, Crow weaves. Tyres skid as he pulls hard across the stones to dodge a bluff of lads in army fatigues, a sprawl of drag queens, a troupe of skull-faced things on stilts. Crow's heart heaves and shunts at each turn.

Hard right. Hope Street. Home straight.

Faster.

Crow shifts up a gear. Shifts up another. Throws weight on the pedals as if jumping. Downhill is not enough. He's overtaking gravity.

Crow starts to see it: a slight delay. A white light ghosting at the edges of the buildings, car windows reflecting the headlights of some oncoming unknown. In place of his walkie-talkie Crow feels the tarot deck burn through his shoulder strap.

The trick is this: start the race with a full deck and you never have to stop.

Finch did love a shortcut.

The road is a mess. Gouges in the tarmac expose wires under puddles. Too fast, too fast to dodge. Yank the handles, bunny-hop. His back wheel skids on landing but something pulls it upright, slides him back to centre. Some dark hand fixes him to a path, a destination. No time to form thoughts of who might be steering.

A bus, forty-nine grumbling feet and three inches of impending pain, pulls out of St Vincent Street to stretch across Hope. True to form there's Remmy, gliding alongside.

The invisible steering force lifts. Crow veers sideways, a jumped stylus. The slow-turning bus and Remmy's bearded face blur past. Remmy shouts something encouraging – 'That's more like it!' – but the dark, the rain, the blaring car horns swallow him up.

A vanishing point appears at the foot of Hope Street. Crow should be able to see the Hielanman's Umbrella but there's a fold in the world, a crease in the map. Ghost lights run in streaks, anchored to a horizon too close. Far too close.

It was a crazy thing, to belong to a life with more locked doors than open roads; crazier still to be on the other side. Finch had been a shortcut, a cheat, a red-light run.

And now the world is flickering, fluxing, flickering out.

Crow had known, of course he had, from that first night, falling for Finch would wreck him. Waiting for someone like that to return from the unknown? Better to follow, whatever the risk.

No more faulty planning. No more pedestrian crossings. No more safety lanes. No more wrong-way one-way streets.

Unknown routes converge. Life unfolds once more, and a great nothing consumes Crow. Something close to completion.

Nowhere becomes his destination.

His handlebars vanish, then his wheels.

Then so does he.

Heavy rain falls on cracked Hope Street.

Lynnda Wardle

JOHANNESBURG MEMOIR: THREE FRAGMENTS

I

She and me and foursquare walls. I am in their life now. New baby in number twofourtwo Acacia Gardens. She and me. We look at each other; my blue eye; hers. We are as big as the sky our world so round and full of each other. Alone together we circle. When she looks at me she leans. Over and over her blue eye swallows mine. It is the eye of love. How do I know this? Her blue gaze, a soft arm to scoop me up. I am. I am the perfect baby, a creature with the chance to be anything.

Then she is gone. Sudden blank of space no sign. Where is she? My eyes track the room – white white white picture of. Light above, glass and hum. Where? Come back don't go. Where is she? Gone? Will she come back? The place of missing her is already deep, the tree uprooted before it can take hold. I remember this missing but only as a feeling in my belly like hunger. I cry. It must be hungry. It works. With the thin vibrate and teary cheeks I pull her back, yes! And her face looms over me again. Another face there in the centre of her eye, small so small. It is me. I am. The whole world over me. All that is everything is here in her and me and the blue blue eye. The sky from east to west in her soft freckled skin and hair falling on either side. Sometimes tickle. The light behind her bright edges, her lips pink and teeth spitwet. Lalalala o little baby, toela toela, she sings. Her tongue clicks, rolling in her dark mouth. Mamamama she. Smacking her lips. Terrifying and lovely. Mamamaa. I will try and do this too but it is not right. We will do this day after day until one day I make the noise that pleases her. Mama! Oh Marius, she coos holding me against her chest, pat my little back, so proud she is of the sound. A mamamama.

II

Now I sit fatbottomed and see their feet all around. Brown rug tufts in my hand wet and sticky. Pink toes and black shoes shiny for work. We have to move. She and me have mashed banana. I don't like food. I like milk. I like the bottle suck and suck while she holds me. If she puts me down the milk goes away and that is the end of. I cry. More milk. She away. I cry again. She needs to eat more he says. He looks at me. Look: he has brown eyes not blue. She gives me cold spoon Pronutro mash. Ggggsshh. And mielipap. I'll eat this slurp up with sugar. I want her to hold bottle me and *shhh shhh* but all is changing. We have to move. Pack everything and away we go. Boxes toys clothes pram. Everything. Big white room empty, walls clean and window blank street facing. We are gone gone. Make sure we've got everything. He says, I've checked all the rooms, we've left nothing behind.

III

Hurlingham. Here is outside and inside; I am free and I can go both. I have bucket and spades. I can dig and we are busy. There are builders and piles of sand, grey cement bags to mix and tap-tap and bricks for walls and dig. The sun on the back of my neck and I smile. Smile, he says with camera in a brown leather case hanging from his neck. He clicksnap. Our new house with money from the old. We sold the farm he says, I've got some capital to put this place together. He is swagger with the new house and build it from scratch. She *wrrr-wrrrwrrr* on the Singer every night makes curtains for windows even bigger than before.

I am. Flying – up and down arms wide – this is a bird. Space to fly and fall and hurt. Knees and Dettol. *Eina!* Never mind. Sting of red Mercurochrome and palmful of jelly powder to make it better. Far away. No traffic. At night no cars or sirens for the hospital. Just *screep screep* crickets and night birds. Even an owl, he says pausing in a night story to say, ahh listen now, *whoo whoo*. Picture of wide-eyes owl and I am frightened of eyes that swallow me whole. It's okay, he says, they don't bite. Look says she: birds pecking grubs and seed and sometime wild cats and stray dogs. But no people. It is not like Acacia Gardens where we say hello, how are you and meet people in the lifts, on the stairs. Where they say, Hello little one and rub the top of my head. There are no neighbours here.

We have to move.

Sudden. She crying holding me jig jig jig on her hip even though I am heavy to lug around like this. Why? Where we going? No questions asked. Everything quick quick and pack the now. Whispers around me the *shsshush* of he says she says. What? What is it? I hear. Noises. He says, noises one night after sleep and I get up to see. There he is bold as day. Standing in the middle of the kitchen. He had. He was. Black as night. Bladdy kaffir. So. I. He ran. I grabbed kitchen knife to chase. Across the fields moonshine stubble and run run. He hid and there's no catching them. But not safe. Not safe for a family any more.

Black is nightowls and kaffir knife glint across the veld. You could have been killed Marius. See him run and run breath steam in the cold night, moon silver and knife slice. Bladdy. Got away or I would of. Nothing safe in this country. We give them a hand and they take the whole arm. Whose arm? *Whoo whoo.* Killed I would of. I check we all have arms and legs and nothing missing.

Move and move we go quick as quick night flit. We leave nothing behind.

Greg Whelan

WHEN THE WATER QUICKENS

Morgan Stead has just turned thirteen years old. He is in a state of flux.
He sits up in bed, groggy, dim. He had dreamt of his old house and
all of his friends. Running, laughing, hide and seek. They threw rocks
at all the glass. But then his mother had pulled him from that place,
shaking him, *get dressed for school*. She had been smartly dressed and
in a hurry for something so he'd only had to feign illness for a little
while. *The world doesn't revolve around the Stead men*, she'd cried up
the stairs. He'd held his breath until the door had slammed and then
he'd listened: the crunching of the gravel; the car roaring away; silence.
She'd gone and he'd won. She didn't fight it like she'd used to.

The *Stead men*. He turns ninety degrees and stares at his profile in
the mirror as if it is someone else's. He breathes in, staring at his sunken
stomach. An innie. He would have hated to have an outie like his
father's. *Like a fleshy thimble*, his mum had said, years ago. She had
been smiling then.

By lunchtime the sun is high and the sky is blue. The air is clear and
crisp in the aftermath of the previous night's turmoil. He had sat up
all night with his head against the cold of the glass, watching the rain
lash at the house and hearing his mother stumbling around downstairs
until she finally slept. It left him so tired that when he had woken
he had thought that he was still at home, running with his friends,
and that this new house had been the dream. But he had only been
allowed that thought for a few seconds, little more.

He gets out of bed and stands in the shower until the water runs
cold. He gets dressed and makes sandwiches from the meats in the
fridge, packing them in his rucksack alongside his mother's flask. Some
biscuits for good measure. He pockets his lunch money and finds
the fishing rod in the garage. Underneath the rod is the box of flies
that his dad had begun to teach him to make. They sit unfinished
and clumsy.

The phone rings and he pauses by the door, knowing that it's his
mother checking in. He knows that she won't call the school, won't

want to speak to anyone but him. Other people make her nervous now. Knowing this is valuable, but it doesn't make him happy. He stares at the strange pattern of the wallpaper, trying not to hear the ringing, thinking that the shapes on the wall look like little explosions. Little house on fire or collapsing. The ringing stops. He makes his way out onto the drive. A neighbour's cat watches him from atop the shed as he tries to kick old mud from off his bike, stuck like tar. It watches as he gives up, licking apathetically at a paw. It will rain soon enough anyway. It is always raining here.

*

He finds a spot on the riverbank where the trees are thick enough for him to feel secluded without losing most of the day in travelling, yet still far enough from the road, the town, the school. The heat rises and swells. Later it will rain. If he actually wanted to catch fish, he'd come back then, but he doesn't. He just wants to be away. By himself.

He hangs his shirt on a branch and rests the rod across a large flat rock, almost too hot to touch. He lies on the grass next to it. One of his arms rests across his eyes, shielding them against the beams that fall through the breaks in the foliage above. The other arm is stretched out above him, lazily spinning the back wheel of his bike, his fingers bumping over the whirring spokes as they pass.

The smell of wetness. The taste. The earth. He's thinking of his old city friends, how they are probably stuck in school, and how they are stupid. Good riddance. He isn't thinking of his father. Of the flies. The knots that were tied, untied. The lines tense, fraying, snapped. His father in the early mornings with a flask of hot chocolate on the riverbank; Morgan casting his first ever line, those arms from behind him, so large against his own, working a rhythm for them both, *like this, like this*, the whirring of the reel. He shuffles until the sun flares against his eyelids, burning the thought away.

He tries to clear his mind completely. To rid his head of all of that, of his mother and her swinging moods, of her muffled tears through the bedroom wall. He thinks about the cardboard boxes that lounge all over the new house, their unopened tops veiled in dust. He opens his eyes to the light and blinks each box away one by one.

He sits up on his elbows and watches the river. How strange and new the water seems. Just like the house, the town and trees. The teachers and the pupils. The accents. All new. But then, not really. They are only new to him. But even the things from before that he had once known so well have become new to him once again. He can't keep up. In school no one seems to know that he is there. And so now he isn't.

He closes his eyes and begins to conjure in the darkness; the dull throb of those chairs; the grainy texture of the blackboard; the dead feel of each page in his workbook. The soft cotton of Miss Clarke's blouse. His fingers run around each button in exploration and one by one they are undone until—

A splash in the water.

He looks up in a daze but there are only ripples left, the echo of an action. Fish jumping in the sun. Morgan tries to picture Miss Clarke's blouse again but the moment is gone. He sits up and yawns. Unpacking his sandwiches, he squeezes the two halves together to make a double-decker. He eats noisily and then throws the crusts of his sandwich to the ducks that pass. He watches as they bicker over them.

Morgan is pissing in the river when there is another splash, heavier this time, too heavy to be merely jumping fish. His body tenses. Something has been thrown. Unnerved, he pulls his shorts up before finishing. And then he sees her, halfway up the opposite bank. A girl. She is younger than Morgan, but somehow he can't place how much younger. With her jelly sandals and beaten sun hat, it's like staring at his mother, aged eleven, fresh from her trip to Ireland, captured and framed atop the mantelpiece. Rubbing his eyes, he shouts across the river.

'Where do you get off watching people without them knowing? Huh?'

The girl is quiet, kicking at the loose dirt of the bank.

'Huh? You little creep. You pervert. Don't you speak? Are you stupid? What's wrong with you?'

She stares at him. He blindly picks up a rock and raises it as if to throw it. She doesn't flinch. Morgan lowers his arm.

'You've peed yourself.' She points across the water at him as she speaks.

Heat roars through his cheeks as he looks down, realising what has happened. He sits down upon the hot rock, hoping that the wet patch will be less noticeable.

'And you've peed in the river.'

'Yeah, well, this is my personal, private, personal space.' The girl keeps staring, the oversized sun hat keeping her face dark. 'So you better – you better just fuck off.'

'It's not your spot. I come here nearly every day and I've never seen you once.' The girl carelessly lobs another rock into the water between them. 'It's not your spot.'

She looks around her feet as if for a fresh rock. Morgan realises that he still has a rock in his hand and lobs it in close to where she skirts the river's bank, spraying water up at her. She stands, unfazed. The ripples permeate, crashing and breaking against each other.

'Yeah, well, I'm here now.' Morgan sips at the last of his flask. 'Anyway, I've never seen you either.'

'I come here to swim at the same time every day.'

'How?' Now he has caught her out. His voice rises in the excitement of it. 'Don't you go to school?'

'No. I look after Mother. She's sick.'

It's a clever trick. He peels his leg from off the rock.

'Yeah? What's wrong with her?'

The girl holds a leaf up to the sun, squinting an eye to look through it.

'She's sick. She stays in bed most days.'

'You don't look like a doctor.'

'The doctor comes twice a week and I look after her all the other times.' She drops the leaf. 'Why don't you go to school? Is your mother sick too?'

Her accent isn't like those he hears around him each day in the new school, or in the streets or shops of the town. She seems apart from them all. Different. He unclenches his fists.

'I do, I mean, no. I do go to school.'

'Then why aren't you there just now?'

It sounds like an attack. The back of Morgan's neck becomes hot. He kicks at the earth at his feet, sending little stones tumbling down into the water.

'What's it to you? Are you going to grass me up?'

The girl slides down the bank on the seat of her shorts, coming into the light. She is older than he first assumed. Maybe only a year younger than him, give or take. He watches as she pulls her shorts off without a thought, revealing a two-tone bathing suit. Stepping out of her jelly sandals, she wades into the water until it is lapping gently at her knees.

'No. And you're not going to catch anything here.'

'What?'

'The rod. You're fishing. You won't catch anything here. Especially if you keep peeing everywhere.'

He chews his bottom lip.

'You should have been here last summer. When it was really hot. There's a creek a little further back and when I came to see it it had shrunk and the fish were up on the rocks and the grass was brown and the fish were drying in the sun.' She laps small handfuls of water up onto her shoulders. 'You wouldn't even have needed to catch them.'

Morgan thinks of the fish on the bank. The impossibility of it. But he wants it to be true.

'I'm not really fishing.'

'Then what are you doing?'

He looks at the rod. Despite the hours that have drifted by beside the river, he hasn't even tied a hook onto the line yet. 'I don't know.'

The girl disappears below the water, sinking to the riverbed. When she returns she begins languidly doing backstroke. Her ears below the surface, she starts shouting at Morgan.

'I can hear the river when I do this. Everything in it. The fish want you to leave them alone.'

'That's stupid. No wonder you don't go to school. They won't have you.'

Morgan draws his knees up to his chin and watches her as she rolls herself in the water mid-stroke, like a mermaid.

'It's not stupid.' She pauses to take another tumble and then speaks again. 'And just because I don't go to school doesn't mean I'm stupid either.'

'Of course it does.'

'No it doesn't. Mother pays for a tutor to come three days a week. His name is Mister Lachlin. Mother says that he is really very kind to us.' The girl pauses and begins to tread water, staring straight at Morgan. 'Tomorrow I'm doing algebra.'

'What's that?'

'You haven't done algebra?' She tugs at her wet tangle of hair like he has seen his own mother do countless mornings.

'Oh, *algebra*. Of course I have.'

'Fine.'

She smiles up at him and begins working her arms in the water like she's making a snow angel.

'When I listen to the river, it's like hearing the blood rush through your ears, but only a million times louder and faster.'

'But the river's barely moving.'

'Well, it sounds how it sounds.'

She sinks until the water comes up to just below her eyes.

'I have to get back soon. Mother will be awake. She'll worry if I'm not there.'

Morgan doesn't know when his mother will be home. She didn't say. But that has become normal. Sometimes she leaves notes, things for dinner. Sometimes she doesn't. Once Morgan had watched her sit in the car in the drive for nearly an hour. She hadn't seemed to move. It had become dark and he had switched the outside light on and then she had come in as if from a dream, pale and ghostly and quiet.

'Don't you have a dad that can help? So you can go to school?'

'No. Do you?'

Morgan looks at the fishing rod.

'Sometimes at weekends.'

The girl runs her hands back through her knotty auburn hair, bobbing slightly in the water. When she pulls her hair back she could be a boy.

'What do you mean? How can you only have a dad at weekends?'

He moves over and picks up the rod. He has never really looked that closely at it before, and its joints and scratches, at what it could tell him about his dad's own childhood. It is suddenly very hot and his head hurts. He rotates the reel arm, the noise sharp in his ears. Turning with the noise still in his head, the heat in his veins, he swipes at the tree, snapping the rod in two. The girl sinks until her feet touch the bottom and then she corrects herself and stands.

'Why did you do that?'

He keeps his back to her and pretends to drink from his mother's empty flask. She watches his shoulders heave up and down.

'Because I wanted to. I don't want it any more.'

'It looked expensive.'

'Why would that matter? It's mine.'

'But why break it?'

'What do you care?'

The soft breeze. A dry rattle from the branches overhead. She returns to her backstroke as if Morgan isn't there, blowing jets of water into the air like a humpback whale. He sits and picks at the balding grass. Minutes pass.

'Come listen to the river with me.'

'I don't have swimming trunks.'

'That's okay. I won't look. I promise.'

Even with the rippling light dancing over her face, her expression does not change. He closes his eyes and begins to lower his shorts.

'It's nothing I haven't seen before.'

He whips his shorts back up, and makes to put his shirt back on, but it snags on the branch. She laughs and splashes as he wrestles with the tree.

'I meant in my Biology lessons. Oh, don't be such a lump. Come in. I'm only having fun. I only ever get to speak to my mother or Mister Lachlin. Please come in.'

She passes back and forward between two points on her back, kicking wildly, splashing the dry bank.

He hesitates, kneading the grass with his toes. He has been at the school for six months and yet this girl has said more to him in five minutes than anyone there has ever done. Taking a deep breath, he tugs his shorts down and runs into the river in his boxers. The unexpected cold knocks the breath out of him. He sits down into the water, gasping. She circles him like a shark, taking in his strange, awkward boyishness.

'And please don't pee in the water. Again.'

'Shut up.'

'Now lie back.' She watches him. Awkwardly, he does so. 'No, like this.'

He watches the way she moves her body and tries to mirror it as best he can.

'Good. Now close your eyes. Listen.'

When he closes his eyes he can feel her bobbing next to him.

'What am I listening for? This is stupid.'

'Shhhh. Listen.'

They float together on their backs, side by side. Lazy rays of sun drift over them. Time passes slowly. When she speaks he can no longer see her. He opens his eyes and watches the trees slowly swaying overhead.

'Do you hear it?' With his ears half underwater, her voice seems to move along its currents, a part of the flow.

'I hear something.'

'What?'

'I dunno. Just something.'

They lie with their eyes shut. A solitary cloud floats between them. The sun draws patterns across their bodies, fleeting.

'The river – I think I hear it.' Morgan's voice is excited.

'I've been hearing it for years.'

They float together in silence. Soon there are more clouds. The air begins to cool. It darkens. Piece by piece, the early illusion of spring slowly begins to fade. The trees once again seem bare, scratching at one another. Above them, the flies thin and the sound of life diminishes. But underwater life continues. Noise surrounds them both. They sit up in the cooling air and float a little closer.

'What age are you?'

'What age are *you*?' A mischievous smile spreads across the girl's face.

'It doesn't matter.'

'No. I guess it doesn't.'

She paddles for her bank of the river. Morgan feels weightless in the water; it pains him to feel her leave. She pulls the battered sun hat over her hair, pushing the wet weight of her locks down upon her shoulders. He steps out onto his own bank. The rock feels cool beneath his feet. His shirt comes away from the branch with ease. He looks at his broken rod and feels regret.

They dress in silence. As he packs his backpack, he hears her struggling back up the verge. He spins the wheel of his bike and runs a hand across the spokes as they pass. He tries to picture the girl's mother, her bed, the room, their house. The girl small amongst it all, like a whisper. But he can't picture any of it.

Even though it is still quiet, he shouts across the bank to her.

'What's your name?'

'Anna. What's yours?'

'Morgan.'

'It's nice to meet you, Morgan.'

'Yeah. Listen, I've got to go.'

'Me too.'

'Bye.'

'Bye, Morgan.'

The rain falls lightly. The river gradually quickens. Heavy droplets push themselves through the spaces in the bare foliage. They bead like spiders' eyes, watching. Before long the rain washes his footprints away from the dried bank and the fish begin to jump.

Morgan turns and sees Anna watching from the top of the opposite verge. She raises her hand. He raises his own hand, the rain running from the tip of his nose.

'Maybe see you here again?'

'Maybe.'

She turns and sweeps the foliage aside and steps into the trees. The foliage falls like a curtain behind her and she is quietly and very suddenly gone. He watches the rustling darkness where she once was until the cold rain begins to sting and numb. He takes one last look at the spot where she disappeared and then edges his bike back up onto the road. With the broken pieces of the rod in his rucksack, he begins the cycle home, hearing the river still.

Sarah Whiteside

LITTLE BIRD

'We don't have clocks in here. It makes the time go faster.' Sister takes the clock off the wall and lays it face down on the desk.

Carrie sits confined in unfamiliar, itchy uniform.

'Done night shifts before?'

She shakes her head.

'Keep yourself busy. It'll be over before you know it.'

Beyond the long glass of the office window, a second nurse comes in and crosses the deserted sitting room, where a TV blares. She comes into the office. The two older women nod to each other.

'How's it going?'

'It's going.'

'What are you on?'

'Third of five.'

'Surviving?'

'Aye.'

'Cup of tea?'

'Oh aye.'

'Better read the files first. This is Catty.'

'Carrie.'

'Sorry love. Carrie. First night shift.'

'What. Ever? Scraping the bottom of the barrel as usual then.'

'The agency sent me,' Carrie says.

This new one bustles round the office, picking up files and ticking things with a pen. 'What are you on yourself?'

Sister groans. 'First of nine.'

'Nine.' She sounds impressed.

'Marge has been signed off for another month and they're not going to send a replacement – no surprise there. And it turns out Yvonne had a holiday booked.'

'Who's Yvonne?'

'The new one.'

'Well then.'

'I could've done without it this week.'

'Is it Colin?'

Sister nods. There's a silence. Both nurses glance at Carrie. The silence continues. They peer down into plastic files.

Carrie says: 'Is there anything I could be doing?'

'Thanks love, that's kind of you.' Sister pauses in her reading, finger poised to mark her place. 'Why don't you go and sit with Mrs Grant in room seven. She likes a bit of company. I usually go. She'll be glad to see a new face.'

Her eyes dart to the dark corner under the desk, then back again. She smiles.

'That's one thing you can do,' the other one says.

'Just don't open the window,' Sister says.

*

Room seven.

Carrie dithers outside the door. It feels impossible to go in. She peers instead through the opening at a white angelic form laid there in the bed, asleep or dead, the grey-white driftwood of her hair spread across the pillow. She'll sneak through and sit there, try not to wake her. She'll sit there all night with an alibi and that way survive until morning, wait for her pay from the agency to arrive at the end of the month and never come here again. She steps forward into the room and crosses it, lowers herself gingerly into the chair between the bed and the window. Breathes out. Glances at her charge.

The woman's eyes are open. 'Who are you?' she says.

'Carrie.'

'What are you doing in my bedroom?'

'Sister sent me.'

'What for?'

'To talk to you.'

The woman grunts. 'Did she give you anything to bring me?'

'No.' Carrie glances at the clock on the wall. Eleven twenty-four. Nine hours and thirty-six minutes to go. She gets this feeling in herself a bit like a film playing. In the film she walks across the room, curls up on the floor in the corner with an arm under her head, and goes to sleep.

'Don't just sit there looking at me,' the woman says.

Carrie scans the room for something to talk about, but it's all generic sunset prints and standard-issue furniture. Even the TV is off. 'Do you like it here?'

'Don't be silly. Nobody likes it.'

There's a silence. Carrie grasps her elbows and waits.

The old woman's eyes are fixed on the ceiling. 'The staff don't like it. The residents don't like it. None of us.'

'How long have you been here? Because you might find—'

'Too long.' The woman sets her gaze on middle distance. But then her face gets a cunning, closed look and she turns to Carrie. 'Could you open the window please?'

Carrie glances behind her at the rectangle of dark, the tops of tall trees that sway out there, a streetlight. 'It's cold tonight,' she says. 'You could catch your death.'

The woman chuckles. 'Catch your death,' she says. 'Hold your breath. Go on, just a sliver.'

'Better not.'

'Why not?'

'Just, it's cold.'

'They told you not to, didn't they. Silly cows. A bit of fresh outside. That's all I want.'

'What did you do before you came here?'

The old woman shakes her head. Her eyes snap shut. Carrie tries to remember the handouts she got on the training day. Person-centred care. Offering choices. Empathy. It doesn't look like enough of a bump in the bedclothes to be a real person under there. Nothing but bones beneath the covers maybe: bones, and her slight breath, coming and going.

It's not Carrie's fault. She looks at the door and wishes she could go out of it. She would walk along the corridor and out through the car park, into the cold of the night.

'What's your name?'

'Mrs Philip Grant.' The old woman doesn't open her eyes.

'Okay, Mrs Grant,' Carrie says. 'It's nice to meet you. I'm Carrie.'

'Elsie,' Mrs Grant says.

'Carrie.'

'No, I mean, I'm Elsie.' Perhaps it's just the light, but it almost looks like a smile, flitting across her face.

The room is full of medical gubbins – boxes of surgical gloves, incontinence pads stacked in the corner. There's little in the way of the personal bits and pieces that usually gather in a living space: no photos, or books, or ornaments – not much of a life.

'You look like someone,' Elsie says. And then she says: 'You're not my daughter.'

'No,' Carrie says. 'I'm Carrie.'

'You're neither one of them.'

'No.'

Carrie sighs. Eleven twenty-eight. Even being in the office would be better. They could give her a nice job to do, folding towels or something. But she can't think of an excuse to go back.

'Why don't you tell me about something you used to enjoy?' She can hear the way her voice has gone. Cajoling. Professional. Desperate.

After a moment, Elsie says: 'I used to like to dance.' And then: 'It was the best way to meet men.'

Carrie almost laughs.

'I don't know how you young people manage now. And don't tell me discos, or clubbing, or whatnot. You don't meet husbands by shouting at men in dark basements. All that din going on. I've seen it on the telly. I know what that is.'

'You're right there,' Carrie says. 'And the night shifts won't help.'

Elsie fluffs herself up and shakes out her feathers. 'I'm keeping you back,' she says.

'That's not what I meant, Elsie.'

'How do you know my name?' But there's something about her face, as if she might be putting it on, this mad old lady act. It's too good. Too good to be true.

'A little bird told me,' Carrie says.

'Little bird,' Elsie says. 'Little sparrow.' And she starts to make this strange whiny noise. After a moment Carrie realises she's singing. She's singing in French, dead nasal and kind of throaty at the same time, like she's been smoking forty a day for years. Brilliant. The song takes off, soaring to its full height, and Elsie's hand conducts, floating on the waves of it.

She stops singing. 'I regret nothing,' she says.

'Is that right?'

'Of course not. It's the name of the song.'

'Did you used to dance to that one?'

'You couldn't dance to that. No. It was all, be down to get you in a taxi honey. Better be there about half past eight. Daft stuff.' She shuts her eyes and leans back into the pillows. 'I used to fly,' she says.

'To what?'

'To fly. I used to fly.'

'In an aeroplane?'

'No.' She shakes her head and tuts loudly. The sound of it pops her eyes open.

'How then?'

'Doesn't matter.'

'Tell me.'

'I used to fly.' She raises her arms to the sides, animated now, palms held out. The sheet comes away to reveal the landslide of her breasts. 'You wouldn't know about that. Not these days. In the embrace of a man, that's what I mean. When the mood was right, we'd take off and float around the room. The band playing a romantic song and my feet would leave the floor. All the couples, floating. We'd compete to see who could get the highest.' Her arms fall to her sides again. 'And now I'm stuck here.'

'You really flew.'

'There are ways.'

'And now?'

'I might as well be dead.' There's a silence. Elsie regards her knees, which shuffle about under the bedclothes. 'What harm would it do to open the window a crack?'

'You can't open it yourself?'

Elsie shakes her head, mouth set in a line. 'I can't manage the catch,' she says.

Carrie goes over to the window, struggles with the catch – which is stiff, it's true – and pushes the window up. She can talk to the old woman about music, she realises. Get her to reminisce, sing the old songs. That way they'll get through the night.

But as she turns back, Elsie is already throwing off the covers in one exasperated movement. Her white nightdress is wrinkled up to reveal terrible white legs, swinging over the edge of the bed.

'No,' Carrie says. 'Please.' And she steps forward to intercept her. But there's a rule about touching patients. She didn't think she'd need to remember it.

Elsie takes advantage of her dither and pushes past. She reaches the window and pulls it wide open.

'Please,' Carrie says again.

Elsie has her knee up on the sill. She grasps the frame with two determined hands.

And now Carrie does touch her, puts her arms around the old woman's waist and tugs. It's like trying to detach a Spider-Man toy from bath tiles. Elsie has suckers for hands, suckers for feet: her wanting is an air lock. But Carrie gets her free, the old woman grunting with the effort, and there's the warm, sour smell of unfamiliar flesh as the two of them stumble back across the room. The bird-bone carcass under the nightie resists, then folds at knee and hip and lands amongst the covers. Carrie also sits. And there they are, side by side on the edge of the bed. Carrie turns to look at Elsie, who is staring straight ahead, breathing hard, but alive and unbroken.

Carrie hears herself say: 'What were you thinking?' She sounds like her mum.

Elsie doesn't look at her. 'You can go home in the morning,' she says. 'I have to stay here all the time.'

The room is cold now. The night air has come in. Carrie goes across and pulls the window shut. She fastens the catch and checks it's fastened.

Footsteps come along the corridor. Elsie shuffles back under the covers, back safe where she belongs – all wrapped up and not going anywhere. Carrie picks up her chair, knocked onto its back in the struggle, and sits down.

Sister's at the door. 'Everything all right?'

'Yes thank you Sister, everything's fine,' Elsie says. She's still out of breath.

'You're very polite tonight,' Sister says.

'You know me.'

'I do.'

'We've been chatting,' Elsie says.

Sister looks uncertain. 'Is it me, or is it cold in here?'

'Yes,' Elsie says. 'We may need something to warm us up.'

Sister gives her a reproachful look. 'I thought you might say that.' She comes into the room, takes a bottle of port out of a carrier bag, and puts it down on the bedside table. She gets a glass from above the sink.

'Two glasses please.'

'You know I shouldn't.'

'Look at this wee girl, stuck here talking to me. She needs something to keep her awake.' Elsie winks at Carrie, theatrical now, then turns again to Sister. 'Just like you sometimes do,' she says.

Sister opens a low cupboard and gets another glass. 'So long as you know this isn't in the care plan,' she says. 'You don't talk about it in the office. You don't put it in the notes.'

'I wouldn't,' Carrie says. 'I won't.'

Sister goes to the door. 'You know where we are if you need us,' she says.

Then she's gone and Carrie pours the drinks.

'That's it,' Elsie says. 'Don't stint.'

'I need it after that.'

'So do I.'

They both drink.

'Can I ask you something?'

Elsie looks at her, poker-faced. Carrie can see what she would have been like as a little girl.

'What was that, with the window? What were you trying to do?'

'You ask a lot of questions.'

'It's my job.'

'No, it isn't.'

Carrie goes over to the window and looks down two floors to the drive and the car park below.

'I was trying to escape,' Elsie says.

Carrie gets this image in her head – a glowing white nightdress, splayed bones and all that wild, white hair – like one of those ancient chalk drawings, imprinted for ever in the gravel. She drinks. 'If you want to leave, you can,' she says. 'You're not a prisoner.'

'I had to sell my house to pay for this.' Elsie looks around the room in amazement, as if she's just arrived here in a time machine. 'I can't go back. I have to go on.'

'Where will you go?'

Elsie considers this. 'Once I got as far as the windowsill,' she says. 'There I was balancing. The breeze was blowing my nightie around. Any minute I'm going to take off. But then I look back and see myself lying in the bed.'

Elsie takes a good swig and holds out her glass for a top-up. Carrie crosses the room and pours in more of the brown, sticky liquid.

'It did give me a funny feeling. It put me off a bit. But next time I'll be ready. Then I'll be flying.' She takes a sip of drink. 'Have some more yourself.'

Carrie sits down and does as she's told.

'You can't see them now, but there are birds out there. I watch them. Watch and learn.'

Carrie's head swirls. She closes her eyes. Some half-remembered music carries her. She dances in her mind. Other bodies also move, close but not touching. It's the way you can work yourself inside the rhythm, become it in the darkness. Then it's more than sound. Before the pills wear off, that moment you can never catch, it's the best of her life.

She opens her eyes. Elsie is looking at her, waiting for something.

'Have you always flown?'

'Always.' Elsie nods emphatically. And then she says: 'Why don't you fly?'

'I don't know how.'

'You'd better learn.'

'I'm only young,' Carrie says. 'I've still got time.'

'Before you know it, you'll be me. You'll be here in this bed and then it's too late. It all gets muddled, like a dream. And now it's over.' She leans towards Carrie, her two hands gripping the glass and something like a smile ravaging her face. 'One thing I've learned,' she says. 'Nothing ever lasts too long.'

*

Elsie drops off first. Carrie rescues the empty glass from the old woman's hands. Finally she drifts herself, head nodding asleep-awake for hours. It feels like the night will never end.

And then here it is, over somehow.

And here she is, still bleary with sleep and alcohol, in the office with Sister.

'I hope Mrs Grant looked after you,' Sister says. 'She's not had an easy life. Husband was violent. Complex family circumstances. Mental health. I say, if she wants to have a drink, what's the harm?'

'She doesn't like it here very much,' Carrie says.

Sister looks up sharply, but she doesn't reply. After a moment she says: 'You'll be back again tonight?'

Carrie nods.

'Good girl. It's not so bad, once you get used to it.' She puts the clock back up on the wall. It's eight thirty-three. 'Almost there,' she says. She pulls out the first file from a row on the shelf and opens it. She pauses, pen in hand. She must be searching for the right kind of words.

It's getting light. Outside the window a flock of small brown birds loop and chatter in the bare branches. Carrie doesn't know what they are. Maybe sparrows. She doesn't know. She goes over to the window and watches one take off. It lands a little further along the same branch, flapping itself steady, balancing. It's like they're living at a different speed: like when you fast-forward through a film to get to the good bits and it makes the whole thing seem daft. These jerky gestures, gunfights, tears – pointless.

She leans a hip against the sill. The mug of tea she holds is warm against her palms.

The bird – her bird – takes off again, intent on something she doesn't understand. Its beak opens and closes and she knows it must be singing, its voice lost in the cacophony. You can tell it's not thinking things through, just acting: doing bird things. It flutters, wing-quick, onto a new branch.

Carrie turns back to the room, to the clock. That's what it's like. You don't know what you're doing it for but even so, you have to fly.

Mary Wight

CATCHING SNOW

tongue catching snow –
the almost unbearable tenderness
in being met

BIOGRAPHIES

James Aitchison's collection *The Gates of Light* was published by Mica Press in March this year. His publications include *Foraging: New & Selected Poems, New Guide to Poetry and Poetics, The Golden Harvester: The Vision of Edwin Muir* and the *Cassell Dictionary of English Grammar.*

Ruth Aylett lives in Edinburgh where she teaches and researches university-level computing, thinks another world is possible and that the one we have is due some changes. She has been published by Envoi, Bloodaxe Books, Poetry Scotland, Red Squirrel Press, Doire Press and others. For more on her writing see **www.macs.hw.ac.uk/~ruth/writing.html**

Originally from Glasgow, **Pamela Beasant** has been living in Stromness, Orkney, for many years. She has published poetry and non-fiction books, was the first George Mackay Brown Fellow in 2007, and has had four scripts commissioned by the St Magnus International Festival, for whom she directs the annual Orkney Writers' Course.

Simon Berry was born in the Midlands, educated in Yorkshire, and worked in Glasgow as a journalist. Has also lived in Sicily and Cyprus. Now he spends most of his time in the Highlands wandering around knocking on doors. His first collection, *A Mask for Grieving & other poems*, was published in 2014 by FTRR Press.

Uilleam Blacker is from Barra, but now lives in London. He is a lecturer at UCL. His stories have appeared in *Edinburgh Review* and *Stand*. He has also co-written two plays for the Molodyi Teatr London theatre group, and has translated the work of several contemporary Ukrainian writers.

Sheena Blackhall is a poet, short story writer, novelist and illustrator. She is also a traditional ballad singer and registered storyteller. She has won several national and regional awards for Scots poetry, Scots singing, ballad writing, and short story writing. She is the current Makar for Aberdeen and the North-East.

Tom Bryan: widely published poet, fiction and non-fiction writer. His work has appeared in *New Writing Scotland* for over two decades. Canadian-born, long resident in Scotland, lives in Kelso.

Jim Carruth was appointed the Poet Laureate of Glasgow in 2014 and is the founder and chair of St Mungo's Mirrorball, the Glasgow network of poets. His verse novella *Killochries* came out in 2015 and was shortlisted for the Fenton Aldeburgh first collection prize and the Saltire Scottish poetry collection of the year.

A graduate of the Glasgow School of Art, **Andrew Cattanach** is a magazine editor who has worked on a number of titles, including *The Skinny*. He currently edits the Royal Photographic Society's *Journal* and writes fiction in his spare time.

Regi Claire is Swiss. English is her fourth language. Her stories have twice been shortlisted for a Saltire Book of the Year award. One of them was selected for *Best British Short Stories 2013*. Regi is a Royal Literary Fund Lector and a former RLF Fellow. She lives in Edinburgh. **www.regiclaire.com**

Ken Cockburn grew up in Kirkcaldy, and now lives in Edinburgh. With Alec Finlay he undertook the road north, a journey around Scotland guided by the seventeenth-century Japanese poet Basho, which led to an extensive blog, an exhibition, and a jointly composed long poem published in book form in 2014. **kencockburn.co.uk**

Graham Fulton's most recent books are *Brian Wilson in Swansea Bus Station* (Red Squirrel Press, 2015) and *Paragraphs at the End of the World* (Penniless Press, 2016). He's the co-author of *Pub Dogs of Glasgow* (Freight Books, 2014). *Equal Night* is forthcoming from Salmon Poetry in 2017.

Lesley Glaister is the prize-winning author of thirteen novels, most recently *Little Egypt*. *Visiting the Animal*, her first pamphlet of poetry, was published by Mariscat Press in 2015. Lesley is a Fellow of the RSL, teaches creative writing at the University of St Andrews and lives in Edinburgh.

Andrew Greig was born in Bannockburn, 1951, and tried to grow up in the East Neuk of Fife. Author of many books of poetry, fiction and non-fiction, he lives as a full-time writer in Edinburgh and Orkney, with his wife, novelist (and now poet) Lesley Glaister.

Brian Hamill has lived in Glasgow since 2009. He currently works as a software developer, and serves as Submissions Editor for *thi wurd* magazine. Brian has had stories published in various books and magazines. He was a winner of the Scottish Book Trust New Writers Award, 2013.

William Hershaw was born in 1957 in Newport on Tay into a family with a coal-mining background. He is now Principal Teacher of English at Beath High School, and has written two textbooks on the teaching of the Scots language in secondary school.

Lucy Ingrams has had poems in various poetry magazines, most recently *Poetry Ireland Review* and *Agenda*. She won the Manchester Poetry Prize in 2015 and the *Magma* poetry competition in 2016.

Alexander Lang has, over many decades, conditioned himself to live mainly in his head, where he has to wrestle with the modern idea of virtual reality, which presents itself when his mind and his computer go blank. This invokes a line adopted from Aesop which reminds him of what he is up against – 'Beware you lose the substance by grasping at the shadow.'

Marcas Mac an Tuairneir writes in both Gaelic and English. His debut collection was *Deò* (2013). His second, *Lus na Tùise*, and a novel, *Cuairteagan*, are forthcoming this year. In 2016 he was named New

Gaelic Playwright of the Year. Based in Inverness, he is a member of the Gaelic male-voice ensemble Trosg. **MarcasMac.co.uk; Trosg.com**

James McGonigal is a Glasgow-based poet and critic, biographer of Edwin Morgan and co-editor of *The Midnight Letterbox* (Carcanet, 2015), a selection of the poet's correspondence 1950–2010. His first full collection, *The Camphill Wren* (2016), is published by Red Squirrel Press.

Jen McGregor was born in Dundee and raised in Edinburgh by Glaswegians. She is a playwright and director whose recent credits include *Vox* (Charioteer Theatre/Piccolo Theatre of Milan) and *Heaven Burns* (Previously … Scotland's History Festival). She likes ghosts, nonsense, bad language and spending time with her long-suffering husband and cat.

Crìsdean MacIlleBhàin/Christopher Whyte is joint editor of the complete poems of Somhairle Mac Gill-Eain/Sorley MacLean and has five collections of Gaelic poems to his credit, most recently *An Daolag Shìonach/The Chinese Beetle* (Glasgow University Celtic Department, 2013). A third volume of translations from the Russian of Marina Tsvetaeva, *After Russia Notebook 2*, is due to appear in 2016.

Lorn Macintyre, poet, novelist and short story writer, was born in Taynuilt, Argyll, and spent formative years on the Isle of Mull, both places inspiring his writing. He is interested in particular in the relationship between writing and the writer's beliefs and personal development. His website is at **www.lornmacintyre.co.uk**

Alan Mackay was born, raised and has lived most of his life in Edinburgh. He is now retired and living in East Lothian, where he gardens and writes a little. Previously published in Chapman (as Alexander Innes) and in The Macallan/*Scotland on Sunday* collection *Shorts*.

David Shaw Mackenzie is from Easter Ross. He lives in London. He is the author of two novels, the most recent of which is *The Interpretations* (Sandstone Press).

Victoria MacKenzie was awarded a 2016 New Writers Award from the Scottish Book Trust for her short fiction. She is writing her first novel, *Brantwood*, based on the life of John Ruskin, for which she was awarded a Bridge Award from Moniack Mhor and an Emerging Writer Residency at Cove Park.

Palma McKeown lives in Motherwell with her musician husband. She has been writing poetry on and off for twenty years and has attended many workshops, but only recently started submitting poems for publication. Much of her poetry is inspired by her family and the surreal (often the same thing).

Ann MacKinnon's poems have been published in *Northwords*, *Chapman*, *Lallans* and the *Herald* and have won prizes including the Dorothy Dunbar Trophy. In 2014 she received a Scottish Book Trust New Writers Award for Scots Poetry. Her pamphlet *Nae Flooers* has been shortlisted for the 2016 Callum MacDonald Poetry Pamphlet competition.

Olivia McMahon, born in England of Irish parents but living in Aberdeen for the last half-century, recently published a collection of poems – *what are you looking at me for?* – inspired by works of art in Aberdeen Art Gallery. She's almost completed her third novel, entitled *Remorse*.

Hugh McMillan is a poet from south-west Scotland. He has been published, anthologised and broadcast widely. His selected poems *Not Actually Being in Dumfries* were published by Luath Press in 2015. His book about his home region, *McMillan's Galloway: An Unreliable Journey*, was published in 2016, also by Luath.

Marion Fiona Morrison – born in Barra, educated in St Gerard's School, Glasgow, and graduated MA from Glasgow University. Gained an MLitt in 2006 for her research thesis, *A Chiad Ghinealach*, which explored the experience of the first generation of Gaelic-medium pupils. She enjoys performing with South Uist traditional singing group Guthan an Iar, and writing poetry.

Danny Murphy, best known for books on education such as *Everyone's Future* (2015), is now focusing on creative writing. He recently won the Costa Short Story Award 2015 for his story 'Rogey', and is currently working on a collection of interlinked short stories, of which 'Crawford' is one.

Donald S. Murray is from Ness, Isle of Lewis, but now lives in Shetland. His latest book is *Herring Tales: How The Silver Darlings Influenced Human Taste and History* (Bloomsbury).

Stephen Nelson is the author of several books of poetry, including *Lunar Poems for New Religions*, *Thorn Corners*, and a book of visual poetry called *Arcturian Punctuation*. He has exhibited and published internationally, and was a contributor to *The Last Vispo*. He recently featured in the *Sunday Times* Poet's Corner.

Niall O'Gallagher is the author of two collections of poetry, *Beatha Ùr* (Clàr, 2013) and *Suain nan Trì Latha* (Clàr, 2016). He lives in Glasgow.

B. D. Owens is an interdisciplinary artist based near Helensburgh. His poem 'An Ear Trumpet for the Earth' was shortlisted for the Jupiter Artland Inspired to Write Competition. In September 2016 he will join the Art, Society & Publics MFA programme at the University of Dundee.

Chris Powici's latest collection of poems, *This Weight of Light*, was published by Red Squirrel in 2015. Chris teaches creative writing for the University of Stirling and the Open University. He edits the literary magazine *Northwords Now*, lives in Perthshire and enjoys a happy addiction to cycling.

Stewart Sanderson received an Eric Gregory Award in 2015. His first pamphlet of poems is *Fios* (Tapsalteerie, 2015).

Caroline von Schmalensee writes technical documents by day, fiction by night. Her short stories can be found in *New Writing Scotland* 30, the *Scotsman*, *The Seven Wonders of Scotland*, *FREAKCircus* and online.

She's has just completed her first novel, an Edinburgh-based urban fantasy crime story.

Andrew Sclater is the author of a 2016 poetry pamphlet by Happen*Stance*. He is a recipient of New Writers Awards from the Scottish Book Trust and New Writing North and was shortlisted for the inaugural Picador Poetry Prize. He stays in Edinburgh, rides a motorbike and builds drystane dykes.

Catherine Simpson's debut novel, *Truestory*, was published by Sandstone Press in 2015. *Truestory* tells of a boy with autism who interacts with the world through his computer. It was inspired by Catherine's experience of raising her own autistic daughter. Catherine won a Scottish Book Trust New Writers Award in 2013.

Morelle Smith has worked in the Balkans as English teacher and aid worker. At Ukraine's Poetry Festival in 2014 she received the Audience Award. Her most recent books are *Every Shade of Blue*, a travel memoir (2015), and *The Definition of Happiness*, a bilingual poetry collection, published in Bucharest (2015). She blogs at **rivertrain.blogspot.com**

Sarah Smith lives in Glasgow and writes fiction as well as working as a tutor and genealogist. She has had short stories, poetry and flash fiction published by Leaf Books, *Duality 6* and *New Writing Scotland* 30.

James P. Spence was the winner of Edinburgh Spring Fling poetry competition 1991. His poetry collections are *The Fatal Touch*, *The Great Escape* and *Oot Thonder*. Scots translations include graphic novel *Unco Case o Dr Jekyll an Mr Hyde*. James has been a professional storyteller since 2002. His book *Scottish Borders Folk Tales* was recently published.

Sheila Templeton writes in Scots and English. She has won the McCash Scots Language Poetry Competition twice, also the Robert McLellan, as well as other poetry awards. She was Makar of the Federation of Writers Scotland, 2010 to 2011. Her next collection is *Gaitherin*, by Red Squirrel Press, due September 2016.

Tia Thomson: living in Nairn, where she found that cottage by the sea! Previously published *New Writing Scotland* 20; Glasgow University graduate, with three adult children, two cats and blue hair. Daft about words, music and Gaelic. Joined ForWords (Forres) writing group 2014 – thanks, guys.

Aisha Tufail was born in 1978 in Glasgow and has lived in Glasgow and Islamabad, Pakistan. She is married with three children and currently resides in Glasgow.

David Underdown lives on the Isle of Arran. He is an organiser of the McLellan Poetry Competition. His poems have appeared in numerous anthologies and journals and his first collection, *Time Lines*, was published by Cinnamon in 2011. A second, *A Sense of North*, will also be published by Cinnamon.

Ryan Vance is a writer and designer based in Glasgow. Shortlisted for the Scottish Book Trust's New Writers Award 2016, his work has been published by Motherboard, Freight and the *Glasgow Review of Books*. He currently runs *The Queen's Head*, a speculative fiction zine: **www.thequeenshead.wtf; www.ryanvance.co.uk**

Lynnda Wardle was born in Johannesburg and lives in Glasgow. She has received an SBT New Writers Award (2007) and has had pieces published *thi wurd, Gutter, New Writing Scotland* and *PENning*. **lynndawardle.com**

Greg Whelan is twenty-eight and originally hails from Methil, Fife. He has a PhD in Creative Writing from the University of Edinburgh and has had many short stories previously published. In January 2016, he was awarded a New Writers Award by the Scottish Book Trust. He currently lives in Edinburgh.

Sarah Whiteside has worked as a writer and community artist in the NHS and in end-of-life care. Her stories have previously appeared in *Northwords Now* and *Pushing Out the Boat*. She lives in Edinburgh with her partner and young son and is currently writing a novel called *Catterline in Winter*.

Mary Wight grew up in Melrose and has lived in and around Edinburgh for many years. She has had poems published in a number of magazines and anthologies.